GLASSTOWN

A Play

NOEL ROBINSON

SAMUEL FRENCH

LONDON
NEW YORK TORONTO SYDNEY HOLLYWOOD

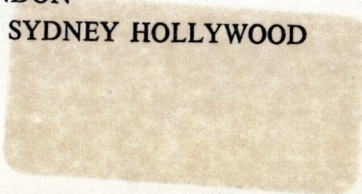

INTRODUCTORY NOTE

The Brontë family was a legend even before Charlotte died in 1855, the only one of Patrick Brontë's six children to live into her thirties. The legends have multiplied since, and the researcher who sorts through the mass of material which has accumulated finds that many accepted versions of characters and events have no basis in anything more substantial than hearsay, or in the case of early biographers, a splash of Victorian whitewash.

The characters in *Glasstown* are the Brontës as they appeared to me to emerge from their own letters and writings around the period of the play. Some people may disagree with my interpretation of the facts, but the facts themselves I have not needed to distort. The truth, as usual, makes the best story. There has been some simplification for the sake of clarity: the dream world of their juvenilia, for instance, developed of course beyond Glasstown into the elaborate empires of Angria and Gondal.

Finally, I hope the style as well as the content of the play will help project the Victorian hothouse quality of life in Haworth Parsonage at this time, both constricting and forcing the emotional conflicts of its extraordinary inhabitants. Although the play is in no sense naturalistic, its emotions are real.

NOEL ROBINSON

GLASSTOWN

First presented by Frith Banbury Ltd, in association with the Cambridge Theatre Company, at the Arts Theatre, Cambridge on 23rd April, 1973, with the following cast of characters:

Charlotte	Anne Stallybrass
Branwell	Robert Powell
Emily	Angela Down
Anne	Vicky Ireland
The Reverend Patrick Brontë	John Robinson
The Reverend Arthur Nicholls	John Rowe
Tabby	Daphne Heard

The action takes place in the ground floor of Haworth Parsonage

ACT I
Scene 1	Evening, June 1845
Scene 2	Night, July 1845
Scene 3	Evening, November 1845

ACT II
Scene 1	Morning, March 1846
Scene 2	Night, May 1846
Scene 3	Morning, two days later

ACT I

Scene 1

The ground floor of Hawarth Parsonage. Evening, June 1845

Most of the set is occupied by the dining-room, which the family uses as their sitting-room, and where most of the action takes place. Other areas represented are the stairs, front kitchen and hall

The voices of the family at evening prayers can be heard before the Curtain *rises*

All Have mercy upon me, O God, after thy great goodness. According to the multitude of thy mercies do away mine offences. Wash me thoroughly from my wickedness, and cleanse me from my sin. For I acknowledge my faults, and my sin is ever before me. Behold, I was shapen in wickedness. And in sin hath my mother conceived me. Turn thy face from my sins, and put out all my misdeeds. Make me a clean heart, O God, and renew a right spirit within me. Cast me not away from thy presence, and take not thy Holy Spirit from me. O give me the comfort of thy help again, and stablish me with thy free Spirit.

The Curtain *rises during the prayers. Charlotte, Emily, Reverend Brontë, Reverend Nicholls and Tabby are kneeling beside chairs in the dining-room*

Deliver me from blood-guiltiness, O God, thou that are the God of my health. And my tongue shall sing thy righteousness. For thou desirest no sacrifice, else would I give it thee. But thou delightest not in burnt-offerings. The sacrifice of God is a troubled spirit: a broken and a contrite heart, O God, shalt thou not despise. Amen.

Branwell and Anne enter through the front door. They are dressed for travelling, damp from the rain. Anne carries a small bag and Branwell two larger ones. In the hall they hear the voices from the dining-room. Anne stands still, bowing her head. Branwell continues taking off his coat, hanging it on the stand, and so on

Reverend Brontë O God, merciful Father, grant unto us, according to the riches of thy glory, that we may be strengthened with might by thy spirit in the inner man: that Christ may dwell in our hearts by faith: that we, being rooted and grounded in love, may be able to comprehend with all saints what is the breadth, and length, and depth, and height. And to know the love of Christ, which passeth knowledge, that we may be filled with all the fullness of God. Amen.

All Amen.

Reverend Brontë Our Father . . .

All Our Father which art in heaven, hallowed be thy name, thy kingdom come, thy will be done in earth as it is in heaven. Give us this day our daily bread, and forgive us our trespasses, as we forgive them that trespass against us. And lead us not into temptation, but deliver us from evil. For thine is the kingdom, the power and the glory for ever and ever. Amen.

Branwell comes to take Anne's coat, and she shakes her head. He goes to open the door to the dining-room, and she holds him back. Branwell immediately sinks to his knees, clasping his hands in prayer and raising his eyes imploringly to heaven, finishing with a great show of crossing himself and kissing an imaginary crucifix

Reverend Brontë O God, who neither slumberest nor sleepest, watch over us for good this night. Refresh us with needful sleep. And grant that when we awake in the morning we may rise with full purpose of heart to devote the day to thy service and ourselves to thy glory.

All Amen.

Reverend Brontë The grace of our Lord Jesus Christ, and the love of God, and the fellowship of the Holy Ghost, be with us all evermore.

All Amen.

They all get to their feet, Charlotte helping Tabby who immediately pronounces in the ringing tones of the deaf what has been on her mind throughout prayers

Tabby If those childer are walking from Keighley in this weather I'll have t'hide off 'em.

Charlotte (*soothingly*) It's all right, Tabby. They won't come now.

Tabby They'll be wanting a proper hot meal when they get in.

Charlotte (*raising her voice a little*) They'll stay the night in Keighley. Come now. I'll help you up to bed. This weather's not kind to your bad leg, is it?

Tabby Out there in the rain. I'll murder the pair of 'em.

Charlotte Warm and dry in Keighley. That's where they are. Come along.

Branwell stops Anne going into the dining-room, motions her back, flattens himself beside the door expecting Charlotte to come out first. But Tabby has dropped her shawl and Charlotte picks it up and arranges it on the old woman's shoulders, while the Reverend Brontë goes straight to the door, Nicholls getting to it first and opening it for him

Branwell Northangerland—where art thou?

Reverend Brontë, coming through the door, starts in shock. It now becomes obvious from the way he holds out his arms that he is almost blind—in fact completely blind in the dim light of the hall. Branwell moves in alarm and the old man's groping hands encounter him

Reverend Brontë There's someone here! Who is that? Charlotte!

Charlotte hurries to the door, pushing past Nicholls, to whom Branwell is a stranger

Branwell It's me, Papa—look . . .
Charlotte Branwell! Papa, it's Branny.

The old man's hands feel his son's face—Branwell stiffening in shock and alarm at the deterioration in his father's sight

Branwell Can't you *see* me? (*He grasps his hand*)
Reverend Brontë My dear son. My boy. (*He enfolds Branwell in his arms*)
Tabby What is it?
Charlotte Anne—my love. (*She goes to embrace Anne*) You're soaked to the skin. Oh, it's too bad. Branwell! I thought you'd have the sense to stay the night in Keighley. Look at her. She'll be ill the whole of her holiday.
Anne (*beginning to shiver*) It's my fault. I wanted to get home tonight.
Charlotte It's certainly not *your* fault.

The others are at the door. Nicholls drawing back into the dining-room. Emily, who has been withdrawn into a world of her own from the start of the scene, now seems to wake up

Tabby What is it? Are they come?
Charlotte (*raising her voice*) Here you are, Tabby. It's Anne and Branwell.
Reverend Brontë Where is she? I can't see her.

Anne goes to the Reverend Brontë

Tabby (*grumbling*) I told Miss Brontë they'd come tonight and she paid no heed. I can make 'em a pot of hot tea at least.

Branwell hugs Tabby

Get them wet boots off ye at once, and your hair dry.
Branwell I don't have hair on my feet, Tabby.
Tabby What was that?
Branwell (*shouting in her ear*) Not in any quantity.
Tabby Yes, darling?
Charlotte (*irritated*) Make the tea then, Tabby, if you're going to.
Tabby I *am* going to, Miss Brontë. (*She goes towards the kitchen*) When they haven't been home for a twelve-month I should think they deserve a bit of hot supper, at least.

Tabby exits to the kitchen

Branwell and Emily exchange some sort of secret handshake or salute

Branwell Well, Major?
Emily My Lord.
Charlotte Emily, take Anne upstairs and get her out of those wet clothes without delay.

Emily takes Anne's hand as if they were children finally allowed to go off together

Emily I've a lot to tell you.
Anne So have I.

Emily and Anne exit upstairs

Reverend Brontë (*gripping Branwell once more*) You will perceive that the Lord has not seen fit to restore my sight.

Branwell turns his face away to avoid his father's searching hands

Charlotte (*aware of this*) Talk to Branwell in the morning, Papa. You're tired now. Look, your hands are shaking. (*She grips his hand herself*)
Reverend Brontë Yes. I am tired. Will you forgive me, my boy?
Charlotte Of course he will. Say good night, Branwell.
Branwell Good night, Papa.

Branwell allows himself to be drawn into his father's arms again. Charlotte keeping her hold on the old man, and drawing him away gently

Charlotte You'll see him in the morning.
Reverend Brontë Don't stay up late. Talking.
Charlotte No, no. (*She leads him off*)
Reverend Brontë You see, I did not know who it was in the dark.
Charlotte Of course you didn't. It was a remarkably silly trick.

Charlotte glances back at Branwell as her father stops to wind the clock on the stairs

Even for him.

Branwell assumes an exaggerated sneering smile and sweeps into a deep bow

Charlotte turns away, resolutely not communicating with him on this level. She continues upstairs with her father and they exit

In the hall Branwell feels his boots, decides to take them and his socks off, and carrying them, goes barefoot into the dining-room. He closes the door before realizing Nicholls is in the room. His manner immediately changes to a jaunty arrogance, the sneering smile returns, whilst shyness prevents him from uttering a word. Nicholls' own diffidence turns him into a stiff prig

Nicholls (*holding out his hand*) Arthur Nicholls.

Branwell nods distantly, seeming not to see the outstretched hand. He goes to the fire and arranges boots and socks in front of it with his back to Nicholls

I intrude—I must apologize. (*He pauses*) I remained because there are one or two matters I have to discuss with Miss Brontë. (*Pause*) I'll call tomorrow morning. (*He turns abruptly to leave*)

Branwell Not at all, sir. No. By no means leave on my account.

Nicholls hesitates. Branwell finally turns and holds out his hand with a flourish

Your servant Branwell Brontë, sir. It's a great pleasure to make your acquaintance. My father's new curate, I take it?
Nicholls Yes. Yes, indeed.
Branwell You're settling down, I trust, among the barbarians of these hills?
Nicholls (*unsure what to make of him*) Yes, I . . . Yes indeed.

Branwell goes to sprawl on the sofa, waving Nicholls in a lordly way to a chair

Branwell Ours is a small hamlet, sir, isolated from the great world, rude in manners, and deficient in elegance, taste, scholarship, the finer feelings and the loftier realms of art. But my childhood home, sir. And therefore never quite eradicated from my consciousness. "Where e'er I roam, whatever realms to see, My heart untravelled fondly turns to thee." Oliver Goldsmith. However much the ways of the great world become my ways—wealth and preferment threaten—for such things do threaten, sir—do you agree?—one gets on, as the expression has it—*si possis recte* —by honest means, if possible.

Charlotte comes in while Branwell is talking, her glance going directly to his bare feet

Charlotte (*interrupting*) Where are your stockings?
Branwell Getting dry, I hope.

Charlotte exclaims irritably as she sees the stockings and boots by the fire. She goes to clear them

(*Imperiously*) Leave them! (*To Nicholls*) My late aunt, sir, in common with John Wesley whom she much admired, believed tidiness was next to godliness and the iron thus entered my sister's soul at an early age.

Charlotte glances at him, as if he has hit on a tender nerve, but leaves the things by the fire. She goes to look in her work-basket

I speak no ill of my aunt. Maiden lady though she was, she took the place of my mother to me for twenty years, and her memory is singularly dear to me.

Charlotte throws another pair of stockings at him

Charlotte These will make you look a little less disgusting.

Branwell holds them up in delight

Branwell How did you know I wanted green ones. How *did* you know? (*He goes to kiss her*) You haven't kissed me, yet, old wheyface.

Charlotte Green was the colour you ordered. (*Slight pause*) Sir. (*She kisses him and pushes him away with both irritation and affection*)
Branwell But such a splendid green. Glowing, yet subtle. I could hardly have predicted that. Do you agree, Mr Nicholls? Isn't that a colour you could celebrate in iambic pentameter? If you were that way inclined, of course. (*He sits down and puts on the stockings*)

Charlotte seems to awake to Nicholls' continued presence

Nicholls Miss Brontë, there were one or two matters I . . . But I can call in the morning.
Charlotte You'll stay and have a cup of tea?
Nicholls No, no. I didn't intend to—I'm intruding.
Charlotte You're not intruding and Papa said you were to stay.
Nicholls (*cooled*) Oh.
Branwell Of course he'll stay. "I love good creditable acquaintance; I love to be the worst in company." Jonathan Swift.
Charlotte (*laughing*) Well, just so long as he makes up his mind one way or the other within the next ten minutes.
Nicholls (*stiffly*) Thank you. It's most kind of you to ask me.
Charlotte You must forgive me, Mr Nicholls. My brother's pitch is too high for me. I am forced to descend a peg.
Branwell Or two.
Charlotte A peg or two.

Branwell gazes at her as if they were enclosed together in their imaginary world

Branwell Clad in these stockings a man might make himself master of the Infernal World.

Charlotte is held by his gaze, half inclined to give way to the old magic

Charlotte That might depend on what sort of opposition he was offered.
Branwell Oh? Are you by any chance planning to put a few regiments into the field yourself?
Charlotte I used to have a certain talent for generalship.
Branwell (*declaiming*)
"Lift, lift, the scarlet banner up! Fling all its folds abroad,
   And let its blood-red lustre fall on Afric's blasted sod:
   For gore shall run where it has been, and blighted bones shall lie
   And . . ." (*His memory fails him*) Et cetera. Et cetera.
"We'll sheath not the avenging sword till earth and sea and skies
   Through all God's mighty universe shout back, 'Arise! Arise!' "
Charlotte (*amused*) What a long memory you appear to have.
Branwell My dear girl, I could reel off a complete list of every army in the Glasstown Confederacy down to the last platoon and up to and including the colour of the camp followers' eyes.
Charlotte Of course you missed out two or three verses.
Branwell They were ill-written. I didn't want to shame you in the presence of a stranger.

Charlotte is held a few moments longer, her lips quivering a little with amusement. Then she turns briskly to Nicholls

Charlotte What was it you wanted to see me about?
Nicholls Oh. The fact is there is a small crisis in the—in the Sunday School. The fever has struck down both the Misses Parrott with one blow.
Charlotte That's a fairly common crisis. It usually manages to strike— with one blow—at precisely the same time as the summer fair strikes Keighley. In this case it doesn't signify, because my sister Anne will be home for a few weeks and we can divide their classes between us. That is, if she isn't forced to spend her whole vacation in bed as a consequence of tonight's imprudence. (*She shoots a glance at Branwell*)
Nicholls If she isn't well, perhaps your brother would . . . ?
Charlotte (*laughing*) Mr Nicholls, you have much to learn. My sisters help in the parish. My brother doesn't.
Branwell You see how I'm treated in this house, Nicholls? My elder sister—once my closest friend and confederate—talks of me openly as if I'm some kind of atheistic monster—some Beelzebub of black iniquity, trailing his coat-tails through the sludge of heresy.
Charlotte I'm delighted to hear that I was mistaken and we'll expect to see you in front of the infants' class on Sunday morning.
Branwell Ah. No, unfortunately I must deny the little creatures that pleasure. I am expected back in Thorp Green by the end of the week.
Charlotte (*genuinely disappointed*) Why? I thought you were both home for the whole time the Robinsons were at the seaside.
Branwell (*shaking his head*) Anne's pupils have gone with their parents. Mine is at home for another few weeks.
Charlotte And you're going back to him?
Branwell Yes, of course I'm going back. I came now only because Anne seemed to need an escort home.
Charlotte She's not ill, is she?
Branwell (*deliberately ambiguous*) No, no. Nothing like that. She'll tell you her plans, I dare say.

Charlotte stares at him, annoyed and puzzled

Charlotte What do you mean?
Branwell (*suddenly accusing*) Why didn't you tell me about Papa?
Charlotte I've told you in letters there was no improvement.
Branwell He's blind.
Charlotte Not quite.
Branwell My dear sister, *I'm* not blind. He couldn't see my face six inches in front of his eyes. You should have warned me. It came as a great shock to me.
Charlotte A shock to *you*? Goodness me. That's not to be tolerated, is it?

Branwell, hurt and a little ashamed, turns away. In a moment, as if in defiance of Charlotte, he launches into full flow to Nicholls

Branwell I have the good fortune to hold an excellent position as tutor to the young son of Mr Edmund Robinson, of Thorp Green Hall, near York, and my sister Anne is governess to his daughters. You know of Mr Robinson?

Nicholls I'm afraid I . . .

Branwell He *is* widely known. A gentleman of some wealth and position. His wife is very well connected. She is first cousin to a peer of the realm and her sister is wife of Mr Evans, M.P. for the county of North Derbyshire, whom of course you know by repute.

Nicholls nods vaguely. Charlotte, desperately embarrassed, moves away

Emily and Anne come downstairs and move out of sight in the kitchen

Mr Robinson is habitually in ill health. A touch of dyspepsia and a large measure of hypochondria is how his medical man described his condition to me, personally. The extraordinary thing is that his wife is not only long-suffering, but of remarkable beauty and sweetness of disposition. I don't think I've ever met anyone so . . . (*He stops*) Anyone I admire more.

Charlotte glances across at him as he speaks, increasingly apprehensive. She goes to the door

Charlotte What *is* Tabby about? She simply had to make a pot of tea!

Emily, Anne and Tabby appear and approach the dining-room. Emily carries a loaded tray. Anne opens the door as Charlotte reaches it

What have you been doing, Tabby?

Tabby They'll want a bit of hot soup.

Branwell "That all-softening, overpowering knell,
            The tocsin of the soul—the dinner bell."

Charlotte (*touching Anne as she passes*) Didn't I hear you coughing upstairs?

Branwell (*to Nicholls*) Lord Byron.

Nicholls (*with a touch of asperity*) Thank you.

Anne shakes her head. Emily capably spreads the meal out on the table, Tabby assisting

Branwell (*to Anne*) How's Old Asthma?

Anne Glad to be home.

Branwell (*to Nicholls*) My little sister shares my emotion on this point.

Anne sees Nicholls for the first time and is overcome by shyness, holding on to Emily as if for protection

Charlotte You haven't met our new curate, Anne. Mr Nicholls. My youngest sister.

Anne acknowledges him timidly. Tabby still fusses around the table

Tabby, we don't have to feed the multitude.

Tabby What, dear?

Charlotte (*loudly*) No need to starve in this house!

Tabby Thou'd never starve, dear. No matter where.

Branwell (*laughing*) *Touché.* (*He looks ironically at Charlotte*)

Tabby What was that?

Charlotte Bedtime, Tabby. (*She takes Tabby's arm firmly, turning away from Branwell*)

Tabby I can get up stairs by me sen. Until I'm carried down 'em in my coffin.

Branwell again breaks into loud laughter, and puts his arm round Tabby

Branwell Tabby, we'll give thee a Great Glasstown funeral. A gun-carriage drawn by black-plumed horses shall transport thee to a secret place on the moors. The drums shall be muffled, and the mournful cortège led in slow march by the Earl of Northangerland and the Duke of Wellington swathed in crêpe up to their noses.

Tabby I can't hear a word thou'rt saying.

Charlotte (*to Tabby*) Off you go then.

Tabby I'm going. In my own time.

Branwell laughs, goes to open the door for her, kissing her heartily as she goes out

There's my own boy.

Charlotte Good night, Tabby dear.

Anne Good night, Tabby.

Tabby exits, Branwell escorting her to the stairs

Nicholls (*nervously*) Who—um—who is the Earl of Northangerland?

Charlotte Who indeed? (*She laughs briefly*)

Branwell returns, closing the door

Branwell Shall I tell you my most terrible secret unspoken fear? To be supposed dead and shut in a coffin, and wake in the dark and foul air, clawing one's fingers to bloody stumps on the eternally unyielding lid.

Charlotte (*irritated*) Yes. You first spoke that unspoken fear when you were ten. And then locked me in the cellar.

Branwell (*laughing*) I dare say it was a perfectly legitimate act of war. (*He turns to Nicholls*) You may not perceive the connection, sir. My sister Charlotte was for some years closely identified with the Duke of Wellington.

Nicholls Oh?

Branwell I don't mean she was in love with him—it was more intimate than that. To come direct to the point, sir, Charlotte *was* the Duke of Wellington. I myself the Earl of Northangerland. (*Pause*) The gentleman looks baffled.

Emily and Charlotte calmly go about serving everyone with supper. Branwell observes Nicholls with the pleasure of a child out to discomfit the grown-ups

Charlotte (*dry*) On the contrary. I think Mr Nicholls has already divined various aspects of the Iron Duke in my character.

Branwell laughs loudly

You two drink your soup while it's hot. (*She pulls a chair out for Anne*) **Branwell** Like the good little children we are.

Charlotte passes bread and cheese to the others

(*Occasionally taking a mouthful of soup*) When I was a child of nine or thereabouts, alone with three sisters in all my infant masculine glory, my father brought me home a set of twelve toy soldiers and inadvertently started an empire. In no time at all they were twelve young men miraculously surviving shipwreck on the coast of Africa.

Emily walks out of the room as he talks, letting the door click shut with sufficient firmness to suggest she is displeased. She goes into the kitchen

Exit Major Brontë. To cut a long story down to the time you have with us, sir, the result of this early adventure was the founding of an extraordinary confederacy of twelve kingdoms, which you may not find in your atlas but whose existence is recorded in innumerable manuscripts, drawings and maps preserved not a hundred miles from where you now sit. Of course the superiority of this country over the rest of the world is that one can personally select the people who live there—an advantage which makes the normal run of society fairly dreary, you'll agree. (*He stares insolently at Nicholls*) And one cannot only meet whom one chooses, but actually assume their mortal trappings. Would you rather be the Duke of Wellington, or Parry the explorer, or a poet or artist or anyone else more gloriously alive than your dull self? (*He clicks his fingers*) Lo! And behold!

Anne and Charlotte gaze at the air in front of his hands as if he has indeed conjured up some mythical hero in the flesh

And when you tire of the rascals—a proper Glasstown funeral and . . . (*He wipes it off with his hand*) Charlotte, a perfectionist, has little graves dotted all over the moors. Little, obscure graves. (*He pauses for a respectful silence*) But let me tell you about the glittering centre of it all, Glasstown itself. We are not untravelled—Charlotte has spent two years in Brussels—Emily one year—I myself have visted London—and I can assure you, sir, that this so-called metropolis came as a bitter disappointment to one who carried in his mind the incomparable image of Glasstown—a city of such magnificence and splendour that beside it Nineveh and Babylon are puny villages.

There is a deep silence, with all three Brontës absorbed in images Branwell has conjured up, their faces animated and happy. Nicholls stirs uneasily as the continued silence makes him feel some comment is required

Nicholls (*clearing his throat*) I used to play a similar little game when I was a boy in Ireland. I had a little model castle and some toy soldiers and I used to make up little stories about—do you know? Imagine I was a page in the castle and—I'd line them all up and send them off to the wars and suchlike . . . (*He falters, and laughs nervously*) All sorts of capers . . .

Nicholls trails off before a united front of Brontë rejection of his small creation

Branwell (*bored*) What fun.
Charlotte (*abruptly*) What were the other matters?
Nicholls The other matters?
Charlotte That you wanted to talk to me about.
Nicholls Oh. (*He puts down his teacup, ill at ease*) I'm intruding on your family party. I'll . . . The money for the peal of bells—it's not important. I'll call on your father in the morning.
Charlotte Just as you wish. (*She seems to be waiting to show him out*)
Nicholls I'll—say good night, then.
Charlotte There's no need for you to rush away without finishing your tea.
Nicholls No, no. (*He gulps another mouthful*) That was very refreshing. Very.

Anne acknowledges his stiff little bow with lowered head

Branwell Good night, Mr er . . . (*He hesitates as if he has mislaid the name*)

Charlotte opens the door for Nicholls and follows him out through the hall to the front door

Charlotte Good night, Mr Nicholls.
Nicholls Good night, Miss Brontë. (*Hesitating*) I'm sorry I—intruded.
Charlotte We are a parsonage, Mr Nicholls. There was no intrusion.
Nicholls (*chilled*) Oh. I see. No . . .

Nicholls hesitates a moment, struck dumb, then goes out abruptly

Charlotte closes and bolts the door, then goes to the kitchen

Charlotte Emily?

Emily comes through from the back kitchen

You can forsake the superior company of the dogs.
Emily I'm perfectly content.
Charlotte I'll see if Papa is all right.

Charlotte goes upstairs

In the dining-room, Anne continues to eat in silence with downcast eyes, Branwell watching her with amusement. Finally he speaks

Branwell Well?

Anne raises her head to look at him. Branwell pretends to stagger back, almost overturning his chair, as he hides his face with his arm

No, no—turn those basilisk eyes away, I beg of you!

Anne returns to her meal

(*Normally*) Have you made a decision yet?

Anne I made it before I left Thorp Green.

Branwell Oh? I thought you were wrestling with it like Lucifer all the long silent way home.

Anne says nothing. Pause

Am I to be allowed to know what it is?

Anne You know what it is without my telling you.

Branwell I swear I don't. (*Pause*) Am I to tell Lydia—I beg your pardon, Mrs Robinson—that she must seek a new governess?

Anne I have told her.

Branwell Have you indeed! Nobody told me!

Anne I wrote to her at the seaside. She will get the letter when they arrive.

Branwell (*standing up with sudden energy*) Well, I'll be D-dash-dash-N-E-D. What a secretive little mousie it is. (*He stands behind her chair, smoothing back her hair with a kind of patronizing affection*) So I'm to be left to go to perdition unchecked. (*He laughs, full of the joys of life. He strides to the door, flinging it open. Shouting*) Charlotte! Charlotte, come here!

Charlotte comes quickly downstairs

Charlotte Whisht! Papa's asleep.

Branwell Anne has something of tremendous import to tell you.

Charlotte, irritated, pushes him back in the dining-room, closing the door behind them

Charlotte I won't have him disturbed. You remember that, please, while you're home this time.

Branwell Now don't glower like that, just when you're about to be told some good news. Go on, Annie!

Charlotte What do you mean by good news?

Anne Where's Emily?

Branwell Didn't you tell her upstairs? I thought you'd pour it all out in one great gush.

Anne No.

Branwell strides to the door

Charlotte (*quietly*) If you shout again I'll have your liver for breakfast.

Branwell It's pickled, you know.
Charlotte I'm aware of that.

Branwell opens the door with elaborate quietness

Branwell (*whispers*) Emily.
Charlotte Go and fetch her, please.
Branwell (*pulling his forelock*) Aye, ma'am. (*He tiptoes out and goes across to the kitchen*)
Charlotte Has he been behaving himself?

Anne sits silent and miserable, Charlotte looking at her searchingly

I see.
Anne (*stumbling*) No—I didn't mean . . . You *don't* see, you see.

Charlotte lays her hand on Anne's

Charlotte He's lasted longer in this situation than any of the others. That's your doing.

In a moment Anne withdraws her hand under pretext of getting her handkerchief. In the kitchen Branwell puts on an elaborate show of mime for Emily, pointing to his tongue as if some edict forbids him to use it. Emily responds in kind, and they hold a dumb show conversation in the practised manner of those who have played this game since childhood. Finally he takes her hand and leads her to the dining-room

Branwell My eloquence persuaded her to come.

Emily sits beside Anne

Charlotte (*to Anne*) Now we're all here. Quietly listening.

Charlotte taps the chair for Branwell to sit, which he does with exaggerated haste. Anne is rendered inarticulate. Pause

Branwell You've not changed your mind, m'dear?
Anne I've left Thorp Green.

Emily's face lights up with pleasure

Charlotte (*abruptly*) For good?
Anne (*her voice remaining flat*) Yes.

Emily takes Anne's hand. Anne moves towards her and they embrace

(*In relief*) I wanted to tell you upstairs. I've been wanting to tell you.

Branwell watches Charlotte, as the implications of the news dawn upon her like a glimpse of freedom, quickly repressed. She goes round the table to kiss Anne

Charlotte You'll be content to stay home? Enough of governessing for a while?
Anne I don't think I'm very good at it.
Charlotte Oh, my love, who is? Sitting in the corner of a drawing-room

ignored by the gentry and despised by the servants. Or upstairs in a stuffy school room with the doting Mama's spoiled little blockheads. (*Suddenly she is carefree*) Oh, why is there never any air in a classroom?

Branwell Not even in a Belgian classroom.

Charlotte Do you remember our dangerous game in Brussels, Emily? Trying to unfasten the window a fraction whilst keeping the shocking aroma of fresh air a secret from Madame Heger. The pink chalk lady. When I was in charge of a class myself after you left I threw both windows open on the first day of spring. Consternation amongst the young ladies of Belgium! "Mais non, Mademoiselle! Ma coiffure! Que le vent est fort!" And Monsieur stalked in and delivered a lecture on the eccentricities of *les Anglaises*, and slammed one of the windows shut as if my head were in it and then—left the other one open! (*She laughs, stopping herself abruptly*) No, of course you must stay home. Papa will be delighted.

Emily starts to clear the table

Anne I want to earn my own living but not at the cost of . . . (*She trails off*)

Branwell The cost of what?

Anne stares at him and away

Has young Edmund been threatening your virtue? I'll speak to that lad. It's something to do with his adolescence. (*He laughs as if his wit is on a plane beyond his sisters*) But I dare say it is not the virginity of the body that is threatened but of the *soul*—a far more serious matter.

Charlotte (*to Emily*) What date is the Sunday School picnic?

Emily Two weeks on Saturday.

Charlotte I shall need to be here.

Emily The sky won't fall if you're not.

Charlotte I wonder if Mr Nicholls could manage on his own.

Branwell (*in a broad Irish accent*) "I apologize if—if I—intrude."

Charlotte Papa quite likes him and he reads tolerably well. He's better than the last specimen at any rate.

Emily Much as a donkey is an improvement on a jackass.

Branwell laughs

Charlotte Of course if he was invited to tea with a dissenter it would unhinge him for a week.

Branwell's laughter stimulates her own rising excitement

Do you know what he said to me last week? There was a wretched woman they thought drowned herself and her infant. I said to him there's no proof she killed herself. But what if she did, he said, and we gave her full burial rites and interred her side by side with honest decent Christians? (*She joins Branwell's laughter*) Sometimes I feel we're all being suffocated here

Emily starts to clear the cloth

Emily Go to Ellen for a visit and we shall all feel the benefit.

Charlotte Very well. I *shall* go. Now Anne's home.

Branwell Spread your wings! Fly away!

Charlotte *You're* not leaving the Robinsons, I take it?

Branwell Good God, no. (*He looks across at Anne*) Look at poor old misery over there.

Anne struggles a little with asthmatic breathing

Charlotte She ought to be in bed.

Anne I'm quite well.

Charlotte (*pausing slightly*) Well, let us hope they will continue to tolerate you.

Branwell My dear sister, there *are* people in this world—and people of station, elegance and wealth to boot—who find your brother a very agreeable and witty companion. Or so they tell me.

Charlotte Then it's obviously my want of station, elegance and wealth that's at fault. Not to mention my complete lack of that very necessary attribute "to boot".

Branwell A man has no honour at his own fireside.

Charlotte (*absorbed in a recollection of her own*) I remember having a ridiculous conversation about that confusing little phrase in Brussels once. "What do you mean ze boot?" "No, Monsieur. It is *to* boot." "Then it is two boot*s*, Mademoiselle. Even by the rules of your insane language. One boot. Two boot*s*."

Branwell You might be surprised if you saw how I am regarded in fashionable surroundings. Northangerland has his admirers, you know.

Charlotte It was the night we went to the carnival. And Monsieur insisted we speak English, then teased me without mercy on every point that didn't rise to the heights of logic embodied in his own glorious language. And I remember I got separated from the others in the crowd, and he came after me and he caught my hand . . . but there were so many between us, all pushing the other way, until only our fingers gripped and . . . just as my arm seemed about to be torn from me he suddenly shouted out, "Attention! *Les voila!*" and pointed in the other direction, and everybody . . . And then he just drew me to him. "When people are in a crowd they should be handled like sheep, Mademoiselle," he said. "You must remember that in your career as a teacher." (*Pause. She becomes aware of the others watching her and colours, as if she has betrayed herself*)

Branwell (*lazily*) That was the old *rara avis* of Brussels, all right—the great Monsieur Heger himself. Do you still correspond with him?

Charlotte (*shaken*) No . . . Yes. Sometimes.

Branwell Regular bulletins on how to become the perfect schoolmistress. What a worthy profession if you happen to be born minus the creative gift. (*Pause*) I'm writing again.

Charlotte What?

Branwell A novel.

Charlotte How far advanced?

Branwell Oh. Let's say—about the sixth month of pregnancy.

Charlotte Is it any good?

Branwell Schwester, I am but the parent.

Charlotte When can I read it?

Branwell When I come back next month.

Charlotte Oh, so we are going to be favoured with your presence again this summer?

Branwell For a week or two. But of course you'll be at Ellen's, won't you, exchanging girlish confidences over the curling irons.

Charlotte I'll come home when you do.

Branwell Remember I have a witness

Charlotte I'm not in the habit of breaking my word. Sir.

Branwell (*casting his eyes up to heaven*) Spare us, good Lord, spare us. (*In soaring spirits, he launches into a rapid, high-voiced imitation of ecclesiastical delivery*) From all evil and mischief, from sin, from the crafts and assaults of the devil, from thy wrath, and from everlasting damnation. From fornication and all other deadly sin, and from all the deceits of the world, the flesh and the devil. From the burning hill that was ready to fall upon the Christians—from the stones that struck the vital breath of holy Stephen—from the gridiron that fried Saint Lawrence—from the crucifixion, head downwards, that gave apoplexy to Saint Peter—from the fate of Charles the First's head, Oliver Cromwell's nose and Alcibiades' dog's tail—from the impudence of Colonel Blood—the go-and-come virginity of Queen Elizabeth, the death of pretty Queen Mary, the hard-heartedness of Brutus, the clemency of Titus that crucified fifty Jews round the walls of their city. From the Iron Duke and all his bloody cohorts . . .

Anne starts to cry, unnoticed. Emily is again detached, in her own world Charlotte alone matches his mood

Charlotte From the tortuous mind of Percy, Earl of Northangerland, alias Patrick Branwell Brontë—the toast of fashionable society . . .

Branwell By thine agony and bloody sweat, by the mystery of thy holy incarnation, et cetera, et cetera . . .

Branwell and Charlotte face each other in old harmony, Branwell laughing in near-hysterical excitement. Charlotte suddenly sees Anne is weeping

Charlotte My dearest—what is it? What's the matter?

Branwell (*over above*) From all these terrors, good Lord, deliver us!

Anne Nothing. Nothing's the matter.

The Lights fade to a Black-Out

SCENE 2

The same. Night, July 1845

Emily is in the dining-room, absorbed in a large map she is working on at the table. Anne comes downstairs hurriedly. She is tense and nervous

Anne I though I heard her come in.

Emily works calmly, seemingly unaware of Anne's jumpiness

Emily Where are you going? Stay here. I'll just finish this then we can play.

Anne (*coming right into the room*) He does seem quieter now. (*She sits at the table across from Emily, anxious to confide in her*) Sometimes he seems grateful to have me there—and then he suddenly shouts at me to go away . . .

Emily (*animated*) Look—I've recharted all the territories. (*She shows her the map*) What I want you to do is go through all our old maps and check I haven't left anything out. All the explorations. Everything.

Anne takes the chart, her face tense with distress

You might correct my spelling, too. (*She laughs*) Let the game reach a new level of excellence now you are come home. Well then. (*She leans back in her chair, relaxed and happy*) Who shall we be? You choose. (*She runs straight on*) Let's be the Young Sovereigns escaping to join the Royalists.

Charlotte comes in through the front door, calling "Hallo?" as she does so

Anne starts up again nervously, but controls herself. Emily's pleasure has no anxious overtones

There's Charlotte.

She goes out of the room to the hall. Anne behind her. Charlotte is exhausted by the journey, but in an excited, happy mood. She chatters rapidly as she kisses the two girls, is helped off with her coat and so on

Charlotte Oh, it is good to see you. How's Papa? The gig was waiting for me at the station: I travelled in the greatest style. Is Branwell home? My box is at the gate. It's so late I didn't dare keep the poor driver from his bed a moment longer.

Anne glances nervously at Emily

Emily I'll fetch it.

Emily exits

Charlotte No, it's too heavy. Leave it for Branwell. He *did* come back?

Anne Oh, *yes*. Yes.

Charlotte It wouldn't surprise me in the least if he hadn't. Ellen sends her best love, of course, and this for you—(*she kisses Anne again*)—until she is able to deliver the message in person. I've insisted she is to come and see us very soon. (*She holds Anne's hands*) You're plumper and there's colour in your cheeks. A month at home has done you good.

Emily brings the box into the hall

If any of us goes away again, *I* shall. I've been making plans. Why shouldn't I get another post abroad? I miss Brussels. And the language. You may not believe it, but I've been speaking it all afternoon! There was a gentleman sitting opposite me in the train whom I felt so certain was French that I actually got up courage to speak to him. He was absolutely astounded to hear his own language—and eventually I guessed from his accent he'd spent a large part of his life in Germany. Every word he spoke was like music to me. It was something about his face—those heavy strong features. Unmistakable. Even the way he wore his hair.

As Charlotte speaks, Branwell, unwashed and dishevelled, comes slowly down the stairs

Branwell Is that Charlotte? Charlotte?

Charlotte looks at the other two, alerted by the familiar thickening of his voice. Anne goes out to the hall

Anne Sshh. Don't wake Papa.
Branwell I thought I heard Charlotte.
Anne You can see her in the morning.

Branwell shakes off her hand

Branwell (*loudly*) To hell with the morning! I'll talk to her now.
Anne Sshh.
Branwell (*as if Anne is holding him forcibly*) Charlotte!

Charlotte, her mood shifting rapidly from excitement to anger, goes abruptly to the door. Emily goes quietly back to her writing on the chart, and goes steadily on with it as if nothing is happening

Charlotte Come in here.
Branwell Charlotte—I've been waiting and waiting for you to come . . . (*His voice breaks with self-pity*) The most terrible, incredible disaster . . . I . . .

Branwell goes to hold on to Charlotte, trying to kiss or embrace her and Charlotte smartly puts his arms away from her, unable to bear his proximity

Charlotte How dare you shout in the hall like that at ten o'clock at night.

Branwell stares at her a moment, then suddenly begins to cry. Charlotte turns away, holding her hands to her head as if to contain her headache

I'm sorry, I've had a long journey and I've a headache. I can't tolerate you in this state tonight.

Anne takes his arms

Anne He's ill. (*To Branwell, gently*) Go back to bed.
Charlotte He's not *ill*, Anne. Let's choose our words properly, shall we?

Anne leads Branwell upstairs, now helplessly crying

Anne You can talk to Charlotte in the morning.
Branwell Tell her.
Anne Yes.
Branwell Need to *understand* . . .

   Anne and Branwell exit

Charlotte How long has he been in this state?
Emily calmly goes on with her work. Pause. Charlotte stands looking at her for some moments

Emily You must tell us every single thing that's happened while you've been away.

Pause. Emily still works calmly

Charlotte Have any letters come for me?
Emily Mm?
Charlotte Letters. Are there any for me?

Emily keeps her face averted from Charlotte's inevitable disappointment
Emily No.

Pause. Charlotte, her face now strained and tired, is turned away from Emily. Emily raises her head and looks at her intensely for some moments, with unwilling insight into her sister's mind. She turns back to her work before speaking

   He reminded you of Monsieur Heger.
Charlotte Who?
Emily The Frenchman on the train.

Charlotte turns to look at her, taken by surprise. Emily does not look up. Pause

   Anne comes downstairs and into the dining-room

Charlotte (*briskly*) Now how serious is it this time?

Anne is silent, unable to articulate the story she has been anxiously composing for her sister

   (*As to a child*) Let's begin at the beginning. When did he come back from Thorp Green?
Anne A few days ago. On Thursday.
Charlotte And he was in this condition then?
Anne No. Oh, no.
Charlotte He came home well and cheerful?
Anne Yes. Very.
Charlotte Well, then?
Anne I think he had a letter from Mr Robinson. (*Her voice is so low as to be almost inaudible*)
Charlotte (*leaning forward to hear*) From?

Anne Mr Robinson

Pause

Charlotte And that upset him?
Anne Yes.
Charlotte What was in it? (*Pause*) Have you read it?
Anne No, but he . . .
Charlotte He told you what it said.
Anne Yes.

Pause. Anne stares down at the table. Emily goes on writing imperturbably

Charlotte It was a letter of dismissal, I suppose.
Anne (*almost inaudible*) Yes.
Charlotte On what grounds?
Anne He said he'd—found out—discovered his proceedings.
Charlotte Found out what?
Anne He said they were very bad indeed, and that he was to—break off communication with every member of the family instantly . . .
Charlotte But why? What's he done? Found out *what*?

Anne shakes her head miserably

You must tell me, my love. I can't drag it out of you word by word.
Anne (*emotionally*) He didn't have a chance. Ever. There's not one person in that house whoever told the truth about anything. It's the whole family. She's the most disgusting woman I ever met in my life. (*She stops abruptly*)

Charlotte looks at Anne in shocked amazement

Charlotte Who is? Who do you mean?

Pause. Anne turns away, unable to speak

Go and tell Branwell to come down again.
Anne He did want to tell you—he's talked of nothing else but your coming home . . .
Charlotte Then go and fetch him . . .
Anne Yes. (*She stops at the door*) But you see it isn't his fault.
Charlotte I see.

Anne goes out and up the stairs

Charlotte rests her head on her hands at the table. Emily continues with her work, her face absorbed and a little animated

Do you know the strength of this?
Emily (*not looking up*) I don't imagine it's anything to get fashed about.
Charlotte Anne sounded "fashed", didn't she? I've never heard her talk like that. (*Pause. She watches Emily*) What are you doing?
Emily Anne and I have a lot of work to catch up on. We've been very busy since you've been away.

Charlotte With your game, you mean—playing? By "work", you mean play?

Pause. Emily takes no notice

Did Papa let Anne read to him—while I was away.
Emily Not really. He grumbles because it isn't you.
Charlotte You know how long it took him to accept me. To acknowledge his dependence. You have to persevere. He would let her, in time—if I wasn't here . . . (*Pause*) Or you?
Emily Oh, I don't think so. It brings on her asthma.

Charlotte turns away from her, in sudden panic

Charlotte (*strained*) You see she isn't strong enough. I can't leave.
Emily She never has a trace of it when there's just the two of us together.

Anne comes downstairs followed by Branwell, who now seems stupefied

Charlotte Come and sit down quietly and let's talk about it. Have you got some gin up in your room?

Branwell shakes his head stupidly

When will you learn you can't *stun* it, or drown it.

Branwell begins to cry again, leaning his head on the table. For a few moments he cries out loud like a child. The three girls are silent: Emily's pen hesitating over her work, Anne distressed, Charlotte's face a mask drained of all hope and animation. When Branwell's fit of sobbing diminishes, Charlotte speaks

Now what's it all about?

Branwell shakes his head, unable to talk

May I see the letter from Mr Robinson?
Branwell (*shaking his head*) Haven't got it.
Charlotte Where is it?
Branwell You need to understand.
Charlotte Understand what?
Branwell *Understand*

Pause

Charlotte Why did he write to you now? Why not tell you earlier?
Branwell I don't know. Perhaps it was something young Edmund said when he got there . . . I don't know.
Charlotte What sort of thing. What would he say?
Branwell Perhaps he was a bit—jealous . . .
Charlotte Of what?
Branwell Just because he's the only boy in the family, he believes his mother's life should revolve around *him*.

Charlotte stares at him analytically

Perhaps I said something that he repeated to his father. Perhaps he made something up out of his head. *I* don't know. He makes things up. (*Pause*) He's fifteen. He's not a little boy any longer. She can't be expected to spend her life dangling him on her knee.

Another pause. Charlotte watches him in growing anxiety

You don't understand what sort of life she leads! Tied to this sick, complaining old man, who doesn't have a good word to say for anybody —who detests *me*—and makes it hell on earth for her if she spends ten minutes in company which has any pretensions to gaiety and youth and joy. And she is the loveliest, kindest creature on God's earth!

Pause

Charlotte Why did he say your behaviour was very bad?

Branwell He said it was bad beyond expression.

Charlotte Does the choice of words please you?

Branwell It interests me. Naturally. (*He is gaining confidence rapidly. Northangerland beginning to take over*) Such was her distress and unhappiness it would have been cruelty on my part to repulse her.

Charlotte looks from him to Anne, whose eyes are down on her sewing, desperately unhappy

Charlotte Is this why you left Thorp Green?

Anne is unable to speak. Branwell touches Charlotte's arm to draw her attention back to him

Branwell You see, Charlotte, I couldn't be insensitive to what was happening—between us.

Charlotte (*to Anne*) Tell me. Was it?

Branwell (*his voice trembling with genuine emotion*) From the beginning, she always showed me great kindness. Her husband never liked me. He tried to force me to leave several times. At first I thought her intervention on my behalf was out of the goodness of her heart—nothing more. Then one day, when I was deeply grieved at her husband's conduct to me, her sympathy unmistakably ripened into—something more.

Charlotte (*abruptly*) I won't listen to this grotesque nonsense a moment longer. She's a middle-aged woman with two grown-up daughters. You're talking trash. I won't listen to you.

Emily stops working, and sits with eyes down, unwillingly involved

Branwell It's not trash!

Charlotte Of course it is. What else is it?

Branwell To be in love—is that trash?

Charlotte (*turning away*) O, you don't know what the word means.

Branwell You think I'm still a little boy. You don't even know I'm grown up.

Charlotte I can only judge by your behaviour.

Branwell What do you know of my behaviour? We've hardly seen each

other for years. You were in Brussels when I left the railroad job and
you rushed back there again after aunt's death . . .

Charlotte I didn't "rush" back. I was offered a position—just as you were
at Thorp Green. This is what I mean. You're over-excitable.

Branwell My dear sister, I know what I'm saying perfectly well. I'm not
talking about children's stories. I'm talking about the reality of what
takes place between a man and a woman. Of which you know precious
little.

Charlotte turns away. Both Emily and Anne are staring at them

Why don't you ask Anne? She was in the same house.

*Anne looks down again as Charlotte turns to her. Charlotte stays looking at
her for a few moments*

Every word I've said is the truth. Isn't it?

*Charlotte leans over and takes Anne's chin in her hand, turning her face
towards her gently*

Anne (*painfully, her voice low*) Yes. It is true.

Charlotte stays looking at her a few moments longer

Branwell I told you so, didn't I?

*Charlotte lets Anne go and collects together her bonnet, bag, etc., and seems
about to go out of the room without further comment. Branwell grabs her
arm in a kind of panic*

Charlotte—don't go away.

Charlotte I'm very tired. I haven't even had a chance to wash my face or
comb my hair.

Branwell I've lost my position. I can't go back.

Charlotte What do you expect me to do about it?

Branwell It isn't possible for me to—bear it.

Charlotte (*angrily*) Of course it isn't. When you lie around in bed all day
with a pint of gin or twopennorth of opium. It wasn't possible for you
to bear your dismissal from your first tutorship, or the railroad job, or
the famous London fiasco, or all the other disasters when you applied
the same remedy. You can "bear" it perfectly well if you exercise a little
self-discipline.

Branwell (*his voice beginning to tremble*) You've got to understand, Charlotte. It's important to me.

Charlotte I think I've understood rather too much already. (*She seems
about to walk out of the room*)

Branwell Charlotte, please stay and talk to me. Please.

Charlotte stands without responding

I can't *bear* it. You must see that *I*—cannot endure it.

Charlotte You're not the only one. Other people have to . . . (*She stops*)

Branwell I can't sleep. If I eat, it chokes me. I can't *forget*.

Charlotte (*breaking in*) Find yourself something to do. Put it out of your mind. Go away again!

Branwell I can't put her out of my mind—Holy Jesu! Don't you understand the first thing I'm talking about?

Charlotte Yes, I do! And I'm advising you to find another situation without delay.

Branwell How can I think of another situation when . . .

Charlotte You answer an advertisement. Or you put one in the newspaper yourself.

Branwell Oh, for God's sake, I know how to get a situation without you telling me!

Charlotte Then do it! Now! Because if you don't . . . I know you, Branwell. It took you nearly three years to reach the point of doing anything after the London episode—and then only because Aunt gave you more money. But this time Aunt's not here and Papa can't look after you any more. You'll *be* here—month after month—and nobody else will be able to go away either.

Branwell You don't understand, do you? It isn't just losing my situation—it's different this time.

Charlotte Then that's all the more reason to get your mind off it. Concentrate on something else. *Go away!*

Branwell How can I concentrate on something else when this thing's pounding away inside my head twenty-four hours a day! You don't understand anything at all! She's always, always in my mind. Like pain.

Emily, staring at him in intense unwilling involvement, suddenly gets up abruptly, collecting her papers together as automatically as a somnambulist

Charlotte Do you think other people don't have pain? Life *is* pain. You *have* to endure it—every day. You have to go on getting up in the morning—do you think you're the only one? We *all* have to get through the nights!

Charlotte and Branwell stare at each other, as the Lights fade to a Black-Out

SCENE 3

The same. Evening, November 1845

Tabby and Charlotte are in the kitchen. Anne and Emily are writing at the table in the dining-room. As the Lights come up, Charlotte is just turning on her way out of the kitchen, indignantly querying something Tabby has said

Charlotte I don't know what you're talking about.

Tabby Thee and him.

Charlotte He and I what?

Tabby It's nowt but a bit o' talk in village.

Charlotte I can't imagine why either Mr Nicholls or myself should inspire talk in the village—singly or in concert.

Tabby I dare say there's some folk niver expected thee'd still be here with Miss Anne home five months sin'.

Charlotte I'm sorry if I seem stupid. But what has this to do with Mr Nicholls?

Tabby Th'asked what's said, and I'm telling thee.

Charlotte comes back into the room, closing the door firmly

Charlotte I didn't ask what's said—but since you volunteered a tattered scrap of apparently motiveless gossip I'm afraid you'll have to amplify it into some semblance of meaning.

Tabby *(grumbling)* Oh, I can't be bothered with thee, muttering away there.

Charlotte Rubbish. I'm keeping my voice at a perfectly even pitch—which is more than I can promise for my temper.

Tabby *(amused)* Ay. We know that right enough.

Charlotte Well, so that we don't continue exchanging pleasantries past your bedtime, would you be good enough to tell me what this nonsense is all about.

Tabby *(watching her reaction)* Summer said thou'rt staying in Haworth on account of the curate.

Charlotte What on earth do you mean? On account of the curate?

Tabby *I* don't mean nowt, Miss Brontë. But it's plain enow what *they* mean.

Charlotte is silent for a few moments as disbelief and then anger sweeps over her

Charlotte Well, if summer says such a thing to you again I'll thank you to tell them to mind their stupid idle tongues. *And* your own.

Tabby's whole body stiffens into stubbornness

Tabby What was that?

Charlotte You heard me the first time.

Tabby He's a good enough man.

Charlotte I haven't the slightest interest in him! How dare they say such a thing? *(Pause)* Good enough for me, you mean.

Tabby Thou'rt near thirty and not so pretty as some.

Charlotte Plainer than most, why don't you say? The very model of an old maid.

Tabby Ay, and tha will be an old maid.

Charlotte That's *enough*, thank you. We'll hear no more about it.

Tabby If tha won't put theeself out.

Charlotte That's settled then, is it? *(She angrily begins to do some unnecessary tidying up)* If they knew how little relish I have for staying in Haworth . . . It's certainly never entered *his* head.

Tabby Put it in his head, then. Marriages don't make theirsel'n.

Charlotte The one right and proper occupation for a woman! To manoeuvre a man into matrimony.

Tabby What was that?
Charlotte (*loudly*) I said if the choice is between a narrow-minded curate
and no-one, I'll take no-one.
Tabby Ay tha will. With thy pride. No-one. Look at thee, If th'art not in
love what business d'thee have fading to a wraith before me eyes, and
never a smile out of thee.

Charlotte angrily grabs a knife and chops vegetables fiercely

Charlotte Do you think . . . Do you seriously suppose that I'd *stay* here
because . . . Do you really believe I'd—suffer this way for love of *Mr
Nicholls*!

Pause

Tabby Tha mind me of thy aunt.
Charlotte (*abruptly stops her chopping*) What do you mean?
Tabby (*turning away*) Nowt.
Charlotte I'm not in the least like my aunt.

Tabby collects her things together, a little upset

Tabby I think tha should marry, if th' want the truth.
Charlotte Oh, God preserve us from the truth!
Tabby Ye're all the same—the four of ye—since ye were bairns. Your
feelings were too strong for ye *then*.
Charlotte Well, we can't all marry the curate, can we? What a panacea
have we here!
Tabby Tha even sound like thy aunt. (*Appealing*) If tha could see theself,
luv. It's turning sour on thee.
Charlotte Recommended for strong feelings: one curate—to be taken in
very moderate doses only, or nausea will set in.

*Charlotte puts the knife aside and charges out of the kitchen, coming face
to face with Nicholls, who is being let out of the study by Reverend Brontë.
Charlotte freezes*

Nicholls Miss Brontë! (*His face lights up with pleasure before the heavy wall
of reserve descends*)
Reverend Brontë Is that you, Charlotte? Show Mr Nicholls out, my dear.
Charlotte Yes, Papa.

Reverend Brontë goes back into the study

*Charlotte leads Nicholls to the front door in silence, Nicholls struggling to
find some pretext to hold her in a few minutes' conversation*

Nicholls I—your father mentioned you would know about the prayer
books. Which ones are to be replaced.
Charlotte A prayer book must claim to be very worn indeed before it is
eligible to retire from this parish.

Nicholls Oh. (*He laughs uncertainly. Pause*) He seems a little more cheerful. Your father.

Charlotte I would hardly use the word "cheerful".

Nicholls I meant—by comparison with . . .

Charlotte He can't read. He can't work. He sits day and night in darkness.

Nicholls Only yesterday I heard of a lady of sixty-five, almost as old as your father, who—who had the operation on one of her eyes and now has her sight almost completely restored to her.

Charlotte You didn't mention it to Papa, did you?

Nicholls (*frozen again*) Well, yes, I—I thought to . . . encourage him.

Charlotte (*irritable*) I wish you'd speak to me about these things first. I'm in correspondence with the surgeon in Manchester. When he considers the cataract's ready for operation, I'll then take steps to overcome Papa's reluctance. There's no point in reminding him of it constantly at this stage.

Nicholls I'm very sorry.

Charlotte Why should he have this torture always in his mind?

Nicholls I try to lift the load wherever possible. If I can do more, you must tell me.

Charlotte You do too much already. He feels himself useless.

Nicholls (*very hurt, stiffly*) I'm sorry if he does feel that. I wasn't aware that he did.

Charlotte (*passionately*) How could you know what he feels?

Pause. Nicholls's sympathy overcomes his reserve

Nicholls I wonder if it's possible to involve oneself too completely in the sufferings of another.

Charlotte How does one involve oneself, if not completely? (*Yet she is aware of his insight with surprise*)

Pause. Nicholls stares at Charlotte

Nicholls (*abruptly*) Do you need friends?

Charlotte Friends?

Nicholls There are so few people round Haworth with whom one finds anything in common. (*Awkwardly*) But of course you have your sisters and brother.

Charlotte Normally I have friends here to visit. I depend on my friends. I have an old school-friend called Ellen on whose faith and sincerity I lean as on the church itself. If we can't meet, we can write . . . I have a friend in Brussels whose letters cheer and counsel me.

Nicholls (*rebuked*) Yes, I . . . Of course you have friends.

Again withdrawn and ill at ease, Nicholls turns to go, but stops as Branwell can be heard approaching the front door, stumbling a little, and then fumbling to open the door. Though they both know what it is, Charlotte and Nicholls do not look at each other, or give any sign that they know

Branwell finally gets the door open and comes in, very much the worse for wear

Branwell is about to go right past Charlotte and Nicholls, hardly aware of their existence, but Charlotte makes the mistake of talking across him at Nicholls in a crisp, business-like way, as if it were Branwell who did not exist

Charlotte Anne and I will see to the prayer books, if you care to collect the ones most in need of repair.

Branwell stops and looks back at her. Charlotte makes no attempt to hide her disgust and contempt. Branwell looks from her to Nicholls and back again

Branwell I trust you're not misled by that self-righteous, toast-and-water expression, Nicholls. The truth is that my dear sister here is a veritable Janus.

Charlotte makes an almost imperceptible move, as if to stop him

She has two faces, if not three, and another even longer one for wet Sundays. All the time she's sitting in church with her little hands prissily folded on her prayer book for all the world like the minister's daughter, do you know who she is really? She's the beautiful mistress of some sneering black-souled villain who neglects her and ill-treats her and fathers her bastards—and then casts her off. Oh, there's not just one secret, Charlotte—there are dozens of 'em—each more ravishing than the last—you should read the rich purple prose that's been lavished on them. (*He brings his face to Charlotte's, and she can barely control a wave of loathing. In an exaggerated woman's voice*) "My Lord, your eloquence, your noble genius, has again driven me to desperation. I am no longer mistress of myself. Oh! Do not kill me with such cold, cruel disdain! ..." (*He begins to giggle drunkenly*) Can't recall the next bit . . . Can you, Charlotte?

Branwell moves off towards the stairs, stumbling a little. Nicholls goes as if to help him

Charlotte (*unable to look at Nicholls*) No!
Nicholls You can't manage him on your own.
Charlotte It's perfectly all right.
Nicholls (*at his most priggish*) It's not a lady's duty to . . .

Branwell stops and watches from the stairs

Charlotte Mr Nicholls, it would really be more convenient if you could arrange your visits to Papa at an earlier hour. It agitates him to talk so much before he goes to bed, and he sleeps badly as a result. I've been intending to speak to you about it.
Nicholls (*hurt*) I . . . Of course. I'm very sorry. I didn't—realize . . .

Anne goes to the dining-room door and listens anxiously. Emily continues writing unperturbed

Branwell (*in imitation of Charlotte*) Well, kindly see you mend your ways, sir, for the future. *And* the prayer books.

Charlotte (*her distress near the surface*) You will understand that this is not a very convenient time for—any of us.
Nicholls I understand, Miss Brontë.
Charlotte Good night.
Nicholls Good night, Miss Brontë.

Nicholls exits

Charlotte closes the door on him, leaning on it for a moment, as if to assuage her humiliation. When she turns, Branwell is seated on the stairs, watching her mockingly

Charlotte (*fiercely*) Go up to bed.

Hearing Nicholls leave, Anne opens the door, and stands in the doorway. Branwell and Charlotte are aware only of each other—a nightly battle of wills

Branwell Don't bring your sour misanthropic little face any closer or I'll vomit.
Charlotte I'll give you two minutes to get up those stairs.
Branwell Don't forget I'm bigger than you are.

Anne goes towards Branwell to help him

Charlotte (*to Anne*) Go back in the dining-room, please.
Branwell (*still only aware of Charlotte*) "I do assure you, my lady, these deep stratagems will have no effect upon me."

Anne hesitates, finally does as she's told, not quite closing the door, standing tensely listening. Emily still does not look up, but she has stopped writing, and is in fact unwillingly involved in the scene in the hall

Charlotte You have one minute and fifty seconds left.
Branwell She's like a countess. Of course, her first cousin, you know, is a peer of the realm. (*He describes her face and figure dreamily with his hands*) Stately, elegant, fine-featured—a woman of breeding.
Charlotte One minute.
Branwell Do you know what she said of me? She said I had a natural dignity and grace. Grace—I love that word. "All is, if I have grace to use it so." I wish—wish I'd written that. Try—write that . . . (*Breaking completely*) Oh, Christ, it's six months since I've seen her.

Charlotte suddenly puts her watch away briskly

Charlotte Try *Dis*grace. Milton left that one for you.

Charlotte takes his arm and pulls him on to his feet so forcefully that he is taken by surprise and half-way upstairs before he reacts at all

Branwell You stupid ugly bitch.

Anne, intensely distressed by the scene, turns to the table where Emily has started writing again

Anne Now he'll be ill again for days!

Charlotte and Branwell exit

Emily goes on writing for a few moments, ignoring her sister's distress

Emily (*rather animatedly*) I'm transcribing all the best poems into a separate notebook. I'll only be five minutes. Then we can play.

Anne stares at her, trembling. Finally she sits down, her breathing a little laboured

Anne I don't think I feel like playing . . .
Emily (*genuinely surprised*) Why not?
Anne Emily, I can't think about the game when . . . (*Stopping*) I can't put my mind to it. That's all.

Emily goes back to her work. Pause

I'm sorry.
Emily What about? There's no need for sorrow.

Emily goes on writing. Anne watches her, feeling guilty

Anne It's only that—it seems that all the time we sit or walk or write together, we play at being other people—only to amuse ourselves . . .
Emily What's wrong with that?

Pause. Anne is increasingly distressed by Emily's indifference

Anne It's only that sometimes I want—to talk about other things. To you. (*Pause*) I want to talk to you.
Emily Talk away. (*She goes on writing*) You have my almost complete attention.

Pause. In a moment, Anne sits back, struggling with her breathing. Emily writes on imperturbably

Charlotte comes downstairs and into the dining-room

Charlotte I said Branwell wasn't to be given any money. (*As they make no response*) It's simple enough for a child to understand, surely. The only way to deal with him is to force him to abstain.

Anne tries to speak, but is unable to

Yet I have only to turn my back for five minutes, and he's wheedled a few shillings out of one or other of you and employed it as could have been foreseen.

Anne, too, begins to write to hide her distress

(*Her exasperation increasing*) Even if he asks you for money to post a letter, don't give it to him. Post the letter yourself, or refer him to me, but do *not* give him a penny. (*Sharply*) Are you listening to me?

Emily looks up to talk to Anne as if Charlotte were not in the room

Emily Now that the Civil War is settled, I think the Gondals are going to have an exciting year.

Anne (*in a low voice*) Yes. (*She glances towards Charlotte in distress*)

Charlotte is near tears of frustration at their inaccessibility

Charlotte Can you think of nothing else? Either of you? You're *grown women*, and you still play the old Glasstown games like a couple of children.

Anne No, we—we don't only . . .

Charlotte What happens to these creatures who have no existence outside your two minds is more important to you than what's happening to your own brother—your own father. You hardly talk to anyone but each other. You think of nothing but Brussels. (*She stops abruptly at her slip*) I didn't mean—I meant . . .

Emily (*crisply*) You meant *our* land of dreams. (*She suddenly stands up, abruptly closing her notebooks, though she leaves them on the table*) I would say that if everyone tried to make a little less ado about nothing, we might find it quite a tolerable old world. I manage to keep cheerful and busy. It isn't too difficult. (*She walks out*)

Emily exits to the kitchen

Charlotte moves as if to stop her, then sinks her head on her hands. Anne watches her with sympathy

Anne I think it was Papa—who gave him the money. It's hard for him to understand.

Charlotte Papa always *has* given him the money! When I think how he was sent off to London on his own to become an artist—as if the mere fact that he was male endowed him with all wisdom and protected him from all temptation . . .

Anne (*in a low voice*) It wasn't his fault he was robbed.

Charlotte No, it never is his fault, is it? According to Tabby, I shall end up in a black silk gown, with a front of auburn curls beneath my cap, like Aunt, telling my nieces how many offers of marriage I have sacrificed for their sake. There's still the smell of her clothes in the room upstairs —no matter how I let the winds blow through—something between lavender and sour milk.

Anne (*tensely*) I know.

Charlotte Of course you do. You had to sleep in there with her. (*She pauses*) If I ever married, it could only be to a man so infinitely above me that I would be willing to die for him. And I would never plot and scheme, and pretend to be what I'm not, and play some shabby game to catch him and hold him like a sly Belgian wife spying on her husband. I would go to him open and direct . . . "It is I. I am here."

Charlotte's emotion momentarily overcomes her. Anne watches her, unable to get through to her

You must have some structure, some order, to cling to . . .

Anne But you have it. You have that.   ⎫ *Speaking*
Charlotte Without that, there is chaos   ⎰ *together*

Anne You have the Church.

Charlotte (*crying to herself, not Anne*) But what if you can't believe? If there are times when you lie awake and faint and almost die without trying to believe and still cannot!

Anne I have—I know—I have doubted.

Charlotte If people knew. If really good people like Ellen—if the self-righteous, conventional, respectable, *good* Reverend Nicholls *knew*—what thoughts I have. How far—how very far I am from what they suppose. If I only *wanted* to be what they suppose!

Anne You must write, Charlotte. Write it down and the worst of the pain will pass.

Charlotte I can't write. (*Slight pause*) I write letters.

Anne You were mistaken when you said I only think about the game I play with Emily. I'm writing something else. I'm simply narrating my experiences as a governess—as if I were someone else altogether, and they had happened to her—this other person . . . Because if I didn't write it out in some way—there are times when—I could hardly live with the reality.

Charlotte (*as if she only catches the last words*) Reality? Reality is Branwell being sick before he reaches the privy . . . And you can't write about that.

Anne turns away. Charlotte seems sunk in herself

Reality is waiting for the postman to come. That's reality.

Reverend Brontë comes to the door of his study

Reverend Brontë (*calling*) Charlotte?

Charlotte seems not to hear. Anne leans towards her in concern

Charlotte? Are you there?

Charlotte stands briskly. She speaks to Anne in a matter-of-fact way

Charlotte You're looking pale. It's past your bedtime.

Anne draws back from her as if Charlotte had pushed her away. She begins to cough

That's your tired cough. Leave Emily's things where they are. I expect she'll come back for them. Don't be too long now. (*She goes out to the hall as if nothing had passed between them*) I'm here, Papa. (*She takes his arm*)

In the dining-room Anne collects her things together, her shoulders a little stooped, and goes out with them and upstairs during the following scene

Reverend Brontë Is Branwell in bed?

Charlotte Yes.

Reverend Brontë I thought it was his voice I heard.

Charlotte Shall I read something to you for a while?

Reverend Brontë He's working on an epic poem.

Charlotte Did Anne tell you she finished the new altar cloth—all by herself. I never thought she could do it so well.

Reverend Brontë An entirely new venture. He explained it all to me.

Charlotte (*compassionately*) He wanted some new notebooks, I suppose, and you gave him the money?

Reverend Brontë We must see that he has every encouragement. You see you hold a young child's mind in your hands like a plant—you never hold it back. The problem was not his want of gifts, but their over-abundance.

Charlotte Let's read a chapter together.

Reverend Brontë Charlotte, I would like you to be with me during the operation.

Charlotte I shall be. You know I'm going to Manchester with you when the time comes.

Reverend Brontë I mean—in the room with me—while the surgeon is operating on the eye.

Charlotte (*pausing*) Yes, Papa. If you wish it.

Reverend Brontë I do wish it. Yes. (*His grip on her hand tightens*)

Charlotte I'll help you upstairs to bed.

Reverend Brontë No, no. He needs time to get to sleep. I'll sit here a while longer.

Charlotte I'll make you a hot drink.

Reverend Brontë You see, Charlotte, there was no school I could have entrusted with his education. I wouldn't have him flogged into learning!

Reverend Brontë exits to his study, closing the door after him

Charlotte goes into the dining-room. She sets about tidying up with almost obsessional care. She sets the chairs exactly in place. She straightens Emily's papers on the table. She brings out her own portable desk and arranges it carefully. Finally she sits at the table, opens the desk and takes out pen and paper, etc., and then a smallish box. She unlocks the box with a key she keeps in her pocket, or on a watch chain or belt. In the box there is a thin bundle of letters neatly tied together with some special embroidered ribbon or silk, and some sheets of paper on which she has been drafting a letter. She reads it, at last takes pen and begins to transcribe it

Charlotte (*as she writes*) Monsieur. Les six mois de silence sont écoulés; nous sommes aujourd'hui au dixhuitième Novembre, ma dernière lettre était datée (je crois) le dix-huitième Mai . . . (*She stops writing*) I can therefore write to you again without failing in my promise. (*She reads, crosses out, corrects, during the following*) I tell you frankly that I have tried meanwhile to forget you, for the remembrance of a person whom one thinks never to see again and whom, nevertheless, one greatly

esteems, frets too much the mind. (*She writes over words*) That indeed
is humiliating—to be unable to control one's own thoughts, to be a slave
of a regret, of a memory, the slave of a fixed and dominant idea which
lords it over the mind. Why cannot I have just as much friendship for
you, as you for me—neither more or less? Then I should be so tranquil,
so free—I could keep silence then for ten years without effort. (*She
scribbles out a few lines savagely*) To write to an old pupil cannot be a
very interesting occupation for you, I know. But for me it is life. Your
last letter was stay and prop to me—nourishment for half a year. Now
I need another and you will give it me . . . To forbid me to write to you
to refuse to answer me would be to tear from me the only joy I have in
the world . . . (*She buries her head in her hands in despair. Finally she
writes again*) May I write to you again next May? I would rather wait
a year, but it is impossible—it is too long. (*She stares ahead of her bleakly
for some moments. Then she turns again to her obsessional tidying-up. She
collects Emily's papers together once more. This time, one of the notebooks
falls open, and her eyes are caught by something on the page. She begins
to read, then pushes it aside, her mind unable to grasp anything but her
own obsession. Then she takes it up again and is suddenly absorbed in it,
turning from one page to another*)

Emily enters from the kitchen

*She goes through to the dining-room, sees Charlotte is still there, ignores her,
tidies her papers into her desk. Charlotte looks up, watching her. Emily,
missing her notebook, finally sees it is the one her sister is holding, holds out
her hand for it coldly*

Charlotte It's a long time since I've read anything you've written. Too long.
Emily (*dangerously*) Give it to me, please.

*Charlotte leans towards her in growing excitement and appeal, her mind
working and planning as she talks*

Charlotte We used to show one another everything we wrote. Now we do
    nothing together. Our minds are separate.
Emily Are you going to give me that notebook?
Charlotte Not until I've read it. (*She pushes the notebook into her desk and
    closes the lid*)
Emily I wasn't aware that I gave you permission to read it.
Charlotte Why didn't you tell me you were writing poems like these?
Emily Was I supposed to tell you?
Charlotte Why haven't you shown them to me?
Emily Is this an inquisition?
Charlotte It's real, original poetry. By anybody's standards.
Emily I don't care about "anybody's standards".
Charlotte What I'm trying to tell you is that they are good enough to
    publish.
Emily Am I meant to fall flat on my face and worship?

Charlotte When we were children we all wanted to be authors.

Emily You and Branwell did.

Charlotte We all did. To publish was our one ambition in life.

Emily I don't recall that Anne and I had much say about anything until we broke away from you two and set up a country of our own.

Charlotte Of course we'd have to take all those references out of them . . . (*She takes the notebook out of her desk again*) That should be simple enough.

Emily (*so astounded she laughs*) "Those references" are what they're all about!

Charlotte (*driving on*) We could make up a book between us. People would buy and read it.

Emily You do what you like. Don't include me in your plans.

Charlotte None of us can do it alone. We *can* do it together. This is the whole point, don't you see that?

Emily I'm getting angry, Charlotte.

Charlotte We can write stories, novels. Why shouldn't we make a living out of it? People do. It's a profession.

Emily I've no wish for a profession. Why should I?

Charlotte (*hardening*) What alternative have you? When Papa dies. Are you going to marry some stupid pup of a curate? You can't even stay in the room with them for five minutes without stalking out. A profession sets you *free*.

Pause. Emily stares at her

What *will* you do? Get a situation in a school? (*Pause*) I wouldn't be there to protect you from other people, as I did in Brussels. And I did protect you, I assure you. Do you think they'd have left you in peace if I hadn't been constantly covering up for you? Making excuses for your moods and your silence, bringing the world to you, as I do here—to save you the trouble of going out and being contaminated by it yourself.

Emily (*shaken*) Give me that book, Charlotte. At once.

Charlotte fends her off

Charlotte What about Anne? Does she have to go back to some wretched governess job? Do you want to take her one chance of escape away from her?

Emily stares at her, a little astonished that even Charlotte should stoop to such arguments

How could Anne's work be strong enough to stand on its own? But it would have a chance with yours beside it. (*Pleading desperately*) None of us can do it alone. But *together*—it could be a future for us all.

Emily (*her alarm growing*) For God's sake—I don't *want* to be involved, Charlotte! Will you understand that?

Charlotte We all need a stake in life. Hope, motive . . .

Emily Charlotte! I don't *want* to!

Charlotte We all want that.

Emily Give me my book. God in hell, it's *mine*, isn't it? Give it to me! I
don't *want* to be involved, Charlotte!

Charlotte suddenly opens her desk and takes the notebook out again

Charlotte What *do* you want then? For us all to be buried alive?

*Charlotte throws the notebook on the table and it lies there without either of
them touching it, as—*

the CURTAIN *falls*

ACT II

SCENE 1

The same. Morning, March 1846

When the CURTAIN *rises, Nicholls is waiting alone in the dining-room. Tabby and Emily are in the kitchen. Emily is cheerful and outgoing in Tabby's company*

Tabby Yon lad told me it rained on 'im up on Ponden Kirk way.
Emily *(laughing)* He hasn't set foot on the moors for months.
Tabby He were wet enough.
Emily He probably fell in the horse trough again. *(She picks up a pail and scrubbing brush)*
Tabby Well, the bit of a bath did no harm. Are thee going to scrub upstairs?
Emily *(nodding)* I'll turn out Papa's room if my Lord Branwell deigns to get out of bed.
Tabby He kept on about the wind and the rain.
Emily It was the first sunny day we've had all March. *(She goes towards the hall)*
Tabby Where's that bit o' cold meat?
Emily *(going to the stairs)* I cut it up for the dogs.
Tabby She were saving it for Master's supper.

The postman's knock is heard

(Going to the front door) Well, as it was thee that did it nothing'll be said.

Branwell half tumbles down the stairs

Tabby moves faster to get to the door first and take in the mail. Branwell immediately grapples with her for it, obviously a frequent battle

(Pushing him away) Nothing for you.
Branwell Let me see.

Emily exits upstairs with the pail and brush

Tabby struggles to keep the letter from him

Tabby It's not for thee.
Branwell It says Esquire. Look.

Tabby (*fiercely*) Are thee C. Brontë?

Branwell suddenly grips her wrist so that she drops the letter. He bends to pick it up and Tabby stamps her foot down hard on his hand. Branwell gives a yell of indignant pain. Nicholls opens the dining-room door and looks out diffidently. As Branwell's attention is distracted Tabby gives him a vigorous push away, picks up the letter, hobbles away to the kitchen. Branwell stares at Nicholls as if he is caught trespassing

Nicholls Good morning. I'm—just waiting for Miss Brontë.

Branwell continues to look at him coldly, his hurt fingers in his mouth like a baby's dummy

She's collecting one or two articles . . .

Branwell's stare does not waver

Warm clothes and suchlike for—one or two poor families in the—in the parish.

Branwell How fortunate to be *in* the parish—and not cast into the outer darkness with the other untouchables.

Branwell pushes insolently past Nicholls into the dining-room, goes to sprawl on the sofa. Nicholls remains standing near the door

Tabby disappears from sight in the kitchen

So your flock is keeping you occupied, is it? That is to say, the ninety-and-nine left inside.

Nicholls does not answer

I've always thought it grossly unfair that there should be all that rejoicing over the hundredth one that strayed. It seems that the only way to be rejoiced over is to be a repentant sinner. And to be a repentant sinner you have first to sin. The more the better. The wages of sin are the fatted calf.

He studies Nicholls, who gazes carefully in front of him

You don't think, do you, that the Church is encouraging sin?

Pause

Nicholls (*stiffly*) No doubt you would prefer the doctrine of the Calvinists.
Branwell Ah. Yes, but you see that doesn't work either. If you know you're damned anyway then you may as well go ahead and have your money's worth. (*Pause*) My sister Anne, now, is a prime example of the sheep that never strayed, and nobody has ever given her one single slice of fatted calf. I don't speak for my other sisters—the duplicity of Charlotte's nature I think I have already expounded to you, and Emily of course cares for nobody—except the dogs and possibly the Great God Pan.

Nicholls shows slight surprise

Nicholls I believe we may be certain that all your sisters will find their reward in heaven.

Branwell What? Sitting on a wet cloud with Moses and the prophets? For ever and ever Amen. I wonder what the incidence of piles is in the realms of the Blest. (*Genuinely*) My late aunt was a woman without sin, so far as I know—a touch of rancour, yes, but that isn't a sin, is it? Is it? She taught us to dread the Day of Judgement. And I saw her suffer the tortures of the damned right here on earth before she died. (*He stares at Nicholls*) Her bowels were obstructed. Like a blocked drain-pipe. Let your imagination dwell on that. I was the only one at home at the time. My sisters know all about Purgatory in theory, you see, but I'm the one who's seen it in practice.

Pause. Nicholls is looking elsewhere

We've always thought a great deal about sin in this house.

Nicholls You did right. We all should think a great deal about sin.

Branwell begins to laugh, wagging a finger at him

Branwell Aha. Caught you that time, Reverend. In *flagrante delicto.* "Flee from sin as from a serpent, for if thou comest too near it, it will bite thee."

Nicholls turns away. Branwell lies back on the sofa

(*Pause*) Thought is the greatest of sins. Round and round, like a tread-mill, until the mind droops with exhaustion, the heart begins to strain and pant, the very brain dissolves. At such times, my dear sir, the present of a bullet would be received with grateful thanks.

Branwell looks up with sudden cheerfulness at Nicholls, who is looking at him strangely

A gift that has been offered me, by the way, by my late employer, the incredible Mr Robinson of Thorp Green. There's not a man in Christen-dom who would derive more pleasure from blowing a fellow-creature's brains out. And then calling in his wife, no doubt, and showing her Branwell Brontë sprayed over the silk wallpaper like a spilt bucket of butcher's offal.

Nicholls Might I suggest that if you had an occupation of some kind . . .

Branwell The devil would find less work et cetera et cetera. You're per-fectly right, of course. (*His voice trembles with self-pity*) You must forgive my egotism, sir. I'm very isolated in this house. My family has no understanding of . . . (*He stops*) I have good friends in Halifax and else-where. I *need* cheery company, the talk of my peers. But unless they send me the money themselves, it is impossible for me to visit them! I can't even send a letter without soliciting the charity of my father!

Branwell stops, his distress genuine. Nicholls turns away awkwardly, goes to turn over a newspaper or magazine on the table. Branwell lies back on the sofa with his feet up. In a moment, he resumes quietly

When I was nineteen, sir, I visited London: the city of my dreams. I fell upon it like a starving creature stuffing himself with cream cakes. I ran from the Houses of Parliament to the glorious mansion of the Duke of Wellington. I swept through the National Gallery and felt the power rise within me to paint the greatest picture in the history of mankind. And by nightfall I could do nothing but cry. (*Pause*) The truth is that I don't want to commit myself to any employment at present. There is a certain possibility, let us say probability, likely to occur in the near future which would—obviate the necessity of my taking another position. I can't say more, except that—obviously the natural channel for my talents and energies is literary activity. When this—eventuality takes place I shall be in a position to devote myself to writing without harassment. (*He leans forward looking steadfastly at Nicholls as if discovering that he is worthy of his confidence*) Will you respect a confidence, sir?

Nicholls does not reply, his eyes on the paper, embarrassed by what he knows is coming. Branwell's voice begins to shake again as he speaks

There is a lady whom I love beyond all others, and who returns my love with all the fervid generosity of a full heart and noble soul.

Charlotte comes downstairs as Branwell speaks, carrying a bundle of clothes. She hesitates momentarily at the door as she hears his voice, then walks in

This lady, sir, has a husband, who . . .

Branwell stops abruptly as Charlotte enters. Charlotte ignores him, goes to the table, sorting out the clothes for Nicholls. She is considerably more relaxed than in the preceding scene

Charlotte This dress of mine should fit the elder girl—Emily's will do for the mother. And there are some warm shawls.

Tabby comes in without knocking, and puts the letter into Charlotte's hands

Tabby That's the lot this morning and nobbud else's laid a hand on it. (*She throws a fierce glance at Branwell*)
Charlotte All right, Tabby. Thank you. (*She pushes the letter into her pocket, but cannot resist a glance at it as she does so*)

Branwell watches her intensely

Tabby The postman knows he puts them into me own hands or I'll set the dogs on him.

Tabby again glares at Branwell to emphasize the point as she goes out

Nicholls' worried expression deepens

Charlotte Then a few well-worn garments for the men of the family.

She holds up a long pair of men's woollen drawers, to Nicholls' embarrassment, which she senses with amusement

Don't look so worried, Mr Nicholls. The postman's quite safe.

Nicholls Oh. No, I—wasn't thinking of the . . .

Charlotte I'm assuming this poor family is so destitute they will appreciate even a parsonage's cast-offs.

Nicholls You're very kind, Miss Brontë. I know how busy you are.

Charlotte I'm afraid I spend far too much time these days on purely selfish pursuits and labours.

Charlotte calmly packs the clothes into a bag for Nicholls, as if Branwell did not exist

Branwell (*to Nicholls*) Of course I also have a full-length epic poem on hand, which is absorbing my attention a great deal at present. When I can go to London personally I might perhaps try Henry Moxon—Wordsworth's publisher, as you know, of course—I do have the materials for a respectably sized volume already. But to send a manuscript from here, without intermediary or personal introduction, is tantamount to saying good-bye to it.

Charlotte That should be simple to carry.

Nicholls It's very good of you, Miss Brontë.

Charlotte (*going to open the front door*) Papa's not well today. There's nothing you need to see him about, is there?

Nicholls (*following*) He tells me the operation has been postponed again.

Charlotte Yes. It is fixed now for the summer.

Nicholls (*hesitating*) Then you will be going away for a time—in the summer?

Charlotte (*a little impatient*) Yes, but my sisters will be here.

Nicholls Oh. (*He remains looking at her a moment too long*)

Charlotte (*coolly*) That *is* all, then?

Nicholls Oh, yes. Yes.

Charlotte Good morning, then.

Nicholls Good morning.

Nicholls hesitates a moment longer, until she closes the door on him

Charlotte is a little conscience-stricken the moment she has closed the door, but almost immediately her excitement wells up. She glances at the letter in her pocket, then goes quickly to the stairs

Anne comes downstairs

Charlotte Where's Emily?

Anne Upstairs.

Charlotte (*embracing her*) There's something in the post. Now how shall we organize this? What sort of mood is she in?

Anne She's scrubbing the floor.

Charlotte (*laughing*) That could mean anything. But she'll be pleased. I'm sure of it. You go and fetch her and . . . No, no. *I'll* go and you stay here. I want this to be an occasion.

Charlotte goes upstairs

Anne looks after her, then enters the dining-room

Branwell Hullo, little one. Surprised to see the profligate on his feet before noon?

As Anne glances involuntarily at Branwell's feet on the sofa he swings them laboriously over on to the floor, rests them an instant, and swings them back. Anne sits quietly, taking up her sewing

Don't stop praying for me though, will you? As Aunt Branwell taught you to pray—to an unforgiving God.

He watches her as her hands falter over the sewing

Branwell Mr Robinson is near death.

Anne (*looking up quickly*) How do you know?

Branwell I've had letters. (*Carelessly*) There was one this morning. He won't live much longer.

Anne I am sorry.

Branwell You're *sorry*? I tell you good news—the best news in the world for me—and all you say is that you're sorry! I've been praying, too. I've been praying every day that Mr Robinson might die.

Anne stops sewing

If he was here—in this room—and I might save his life by raising my finger, I would not raise that finger. (*Pause*) And if I had a gun in my hand, and he cried out to me for mercy, begged me on bended knees, promised me his entire fortune, I would not hesitate—one moment— to blow his brains out.

Pause

Anne (*in a low voice*) Do you say these things to hurt me?

Branwell Why should I want to hurt *you*? I say them because they're true. Isn't that what you're always preaching at me? Truth.

Anne (*almost inaudibly*) You'll break my heart.

Charlotte comes downstairs with Emily, whose sleeves are rolled up and skirt pinned up under her apron

Emily waits just inside the dining-room door as if impatient to get back to the important business of scrubbing the floor. Charlotte comes through to the dining-room, ignoring Branwell

Charlotte (*to Anne*) Let's go into the kitchen.

Anne stays bent over her sewing to hide her distress from Charlotte

Branwell (*rising with elaborate languor*) You'll excuse me if I leave you, ladies. I have one or two letters to get off. (*To Emily*) How is the commissariat this morning, Major Brontë?

Emily The porridge is on the stove. (*She sweeps a bow in his direction*) My Lord.

Branwell (*his face registering extreme pain*) I shall be forced to reduce you to the ranks, Major.

Emily (*to Charlotte*) Is the Mothers' Meeting to be held in here then?

Charlotte If we're to be left in peace and quiet.

Branwell (*laughing*) With Charlotte in the chair it looks more like the Grand Gathering of Governesses. Well, *sed fugit interea, fugit inreparabile tempus*. Which, being translated, means time won't wait for Branwellius Bronteio to write his novel, if he doesn't get on with it.

Charlotte (*generally, setting out pen, papers, and finally the letter from her pocket*) I thought it was an epic poem. (*To Emily and Anne*) Come and sit at the table.

Branwell (*his eyes on the letter*) There's only one saleable article on the publishing market these days, you know. The three-volume novel. Oh, you can get other work printed, at your own risk—you might even sell a few copies with judicious advertising and some favourable reviews. But if one's interested in making money, not spending it—if one wishes, in short, to move into the realms of the professional—then one goes quietly up to one's room, planting one's footsteps firmly in the wake of Fielding and Smollett, smokes a cigar, hums a tune and—Eureka! What have we here? Can it be a three-volume novel?

But even Emily has stopped playing, and in the face of their united indifference, he finally gets out of the room. In the hall he freezes, his face tense and anxious, as he strains to hear what is said in the dining-room. Charlotte goes and briskly clicks the door shut. Branwell moves closer to the door

Charlotte Now. (*She goes back to her chair. She is the only one who seems to feel any excitement as she opens the envelope, her fingers trembling as she takes out the proof sheets and letter it contains. Reading*) "Dear Sir: Further to our letter of the fifth inst., we now enclose for your inspection the first proof sheets of 'Poems by Currer, Ellis and Acton Bell'."

Charlotte puts the letter down, unfolds the sheets as if they were Holy Writ and spreads them out on the table. Pause. She glances at the other girls. Anne is still dispirited, Emily looks mildly bored

(*With proper weight*) Now that we are publishing authors, I suggest we proceed in a business-like manner. Let each author check his own poems in order and make a neat correction where necessary. The first is Currer Bell's. (*She checks through the poem, making one or two corrections*)

In the hall, the listening Branwell slowly flattens himself against the door, Northangerland crucified. Charlotte passes the proof sheet to Emily

Ellis Bell.

Emily looks at the sheet for some moments before she takes the pen from Charlotte, who watches her anxiously, glancing at Anne. Emily makes a correction, Charlotte almost holds her breath in apprehension

Emily There only appears to be one relatively unimportant error in punctuation.

Emily looks again at the poem, as if deriving a momentary pleasure from seeing it in print. Charlotte almost sighs with relief

Charlotte Yes? I am pleased. (*Her excitement bubbles up again*) The printing appears perfectly satisfactory, don't you think? The type is clear and not too small.

Emily passes the proof sheet to Anne

Of course there are many decisions yet to be made. The binding—the price to be charged per copy. We shall have to spend some more money on advertising, of course. It will add a little to the original estimate, but that's to be expected. Then we must decide which periodicals should be sent copies for reviews. (*Her business manner slips a little*) I wonder how long it will be before it comes out? Two or three months? Perhaps less. Can you imagine—we might have our first published work here on the table before us—pick it up in our hands—in two months' time?

Emily glances at her a little ironically

Of course, what is of primary importance is that the work should be got up in a manner creditable to both publishers and authors.

Reverend Brontë opens the study door

Branwell stiffens, moving away from the dining-room door, holding his breath as the old man senses his presence

Reverend Brontë Is someone there? (*He moves into the hall*) Charlotte?

Charlotte hears him and comes out into the hall. She sees Branwell but acts as if he is not there

Charlotte What is it, Papa? (*She takes his arm, steering him back into the study*)
Reverend Brontë Were you standing in the hall?
Charlotte No, no. We're all in the dining-room.
Reverend Brontë I thought there was someone there. Has the post come?
Charlotte Yes. There was nothing for you this morning.
Reverend Brontë I expected the new issue of *Fraser's Magazine*.
Charlotte I dare say it will come tomorrow.

In the hall Branwell stays listening

Shall I read to you for a little while?

Reverend Brontë Is Branwell out of bed?
Charlotte Yes.
Reverend Brontë Is he well this morning?
Charlotte Much better.
Reverend Brontë See that he continues to drink plenty of cold water.

Charlotte drops her hand from his arm, glances momentarily at Branwell, he smiles at her insolently. She turns away

Once the addiction is washed out of his system, you see, he will be well again. It is the addiction that speaks, Charlotte—that takes possession, like an evil spirit. He had a disturbed night—did you hear him cry out? Charlotte, I have it on medical authority that nervous people sleep best with their heads towards the North, from polar attraction . . . I have suggested he move the position of his bed. Your aunt always made a practice of waking Anne, when she suffered from nightmares as a child. I don't know if it was wise—should one wake a child from a dream? (*He pauses, suddenly alarmed by her silence*) Are you there?
Charlotte (*touching him*) Yes.
Reverend Brontë He tells me his novel is well advanced. He has an extraordinary facility in writing. His brain moves with exceptional speed— do you remember as a boy he would sometimes write with both hands at once?
Charlotte Oh, Papa. That was a child's trick.
Reverend Brontë (*emotionally*) And was it a child's trick that induced his art master to inform me he was the most gifted pupil he had ever had? Who gave him personal letters of recommendation to the Royal Academy Schools couched in the most glowing terms?
Charlotte Perhaps we all expected too much of him. And were inevitably disappointed.
Reverend Brontë (*irritably*) I'm not disappointed! How should I be? When he's not yet thirty? If you talk in that strain one can hardly be surprised that he . . . (*He stops*) A man's genius can take many years to reach its flowering.
Charlotte Then let us hope he will find a new situation soon in which he will not be able to misuse his talents. Come. You can't stand out here in the cold.

Upset, he shakes off her hand

Reverend Brontë Where is Mr Nicholls? Has he not come yet?
Charlotte You said you felt too ill to see anybody this morning.
Reverend Brontë I didn't mean he wasn't to look in on me.
Charlotte He has been. I sorted out some clothes for him.
Reverend Brontë I wanted him to write some letters to my dictation.
Charlotte I'll do it.
Reverend Brontë No, no. It's parish work.
Charlotte You'll see him this evening as usual.
Reverend Brontë Now I shall be turning it over in my head all day! You do not appear to understand that if I sit in there all the time, in that chair,

in the dark, my mind becomes imprisoned by one subject and I cannot
—be free of it . . . (*He stops*)

Charlotte I'll leave a message at the Browns' for him to call this afternoon.

Reverend Brontë It's of no consequence.

*He turns away—she attempts to guide him into the study. Branwell is still
listening in the hall*

(*Pressing her hand*) Just leave me. I shall be quite well shortly.

Reverend Brontë goes into his study

Charlotte closes the door gently behind him. She sees Branwell still in the hall

Branwell I had a poem published recently, as it happens.

Charlotte I'm delighted to hear it.

Branwell In the *Halifax Guardian*.

Charlotte I'm sorry you didn't see fit to show it to us. Papa would have
been proud.

Branwell It's not the first—nor the last. In this case, for personal reasons,
I used a pseudonym.

Charlotte That's sometimes considered advisable.

Branwell Like a change of gender? Perhaps I should have *my* business
communications addressed to *Miss* B. Brontë.

Pause

Charlotte What was it, your pseudonym?

Branwell Northangerland.

She looks at him searchingly

There is one to whom it speaks directly. Straight from my heart to hers.
And to *him*—nothing. He's never heard the name. (*Emotionally*) The
bare idea of my being able to write anything at all was enough to make
him physically ill!

Charlotte turns to go into the dining-room. He grasps her arm

Don't make the same mistake, will you? I may have some surprises for
you very soon.

Charlotte It would surprise me pleasantly if you were to get another
situation.

Branwell Anything, I suppose—labouring on the roads, common soldier,
whatever offers, provided it gets me out of this house, and out of your
sight.

Charlotte You could find suitable employment if you tried. The railway
would take you back if you showed them you were fit to take charge of
a station again.

Branwell You didn't call the railway suitable employment when I first
went there! You said it wasn't good enough for me. You said it would
degrade my mind. You *cried*. You cried, Charlotte, the day I accepted
the job! I can remember—you crying . . .

Pause

Charlotte That must have been before I realized you were perfectly capable of degrading your mind by your own unaided efforts.

Pause. Branwell stares at her, trembling. In the dining-room Anne stands, alarmed and distressed. Emily is also consciously involved in the scene going on outside

Branwell (*his voice shaking*) Well, I'll tell you this, Charlotte. Someone else has a very different future planned for me. She won't let me rot away here until I'm too old and tired to use my gifts. Charlotte . . .

Charlotte briskly turns and walks into the dining-room. Branwell shouts after her

We're only waiting for him to die!

Charlotte, tense with anger, turns sharply and closes the door

Branwell goes upstairs

Charlotte sits again at the table, trying to control her anger. Emily stares at her, acutely aware of her emotions. Anne still stands in distress

Charlotte Now I'm not going to allow what should be one of the great occasions of our lives to be spoiled by . . . (*Her voice begins to shake*) As every detail of life is spoiled in this house so long as he remains in it.

She is forced to stop speaking. Pause. Anne sits at the table again. In a few moments Charlotte goes on, her voice firm and business-like

Have we completed checking the first sheet? (*She looks at it*) The proportion of errors seems quite low. Nevertheless I think it would be advisable to have all the proofs submitted to us for correction. Don't you agree? For example, this mistake here in my first poem—where they have printed "tumbling stars" instead of "trembling stars"—would throw an air of absurdity over the entire poem.

Pause

Emily Stars are of course far more inclined to tremble than to tumble.

Charlotte looks at her, hurt, but recognizing her mood. She reaches out to her, managing a smile

Charlotte You're pleased, though? It gives you pleasure to see your work in print? You *are* pleased?

Emily gets up abruptly

Where are you going?
Emily I *was* scrubbing the bedrooms.
Charlotte If we write to the publishers now we can send the proofs back by the afternoon post.

Anne Yes, let's get them out of the house in case Branwell . . .

Charlotte Branwell knows nothing whatever about it, and wouldn't care if he did. He's obsessed by this wretched woman.

Anne (*forcing herself to speak*) It's *her* fault.

Charlotte It's also the publican's fault for selling gin and the druggist's for having opium on his shelves. Is Branwell beset by more tempters than the rest of mankind? Is that to be his excuse?

Anne (*in a low voice*) I'm not excusing him.

Charlotte When he stands there coolly saying they are just waiting for him to die!

Anne He didn't say it coolly.

Charlotte It's forced from the depths of his great passion, is it?

Emily I've heard you say much the same thing yourself.

Charlotte I've never said anything of the kind!

Emily That you wished someone were dead.

Charlotte Oh, as a child. I dare say we all did.

Emily No. Not as a child.

Charlotte What on earth do you mean?

Emily Nothing. (*She turns to go*)

Charlotte (*pleading*) Don't go.

Emily stops near the door

Let's write to the publishers together. I think we should tell them about the novels—that we're each writing a novel. What do you say? Shall we write to them?

Emily I'm not much of a hand at writing letters. (*Slight pause*) Unlike you. (*She looks steadfastly at Charlotte*) You have my permission to write to them on behalf of us all.

Charlotte But you're happy with it? The book? (*Pause. A little strained*) I just want you to say you're pleased.

Emily (*deliberately*) I'm indifferent to it. I regard it with complete neutrality. There. Will that suit you?

Charlotte (*consciously controlling herself*) Thank you. That will suit me.

Emily There's just one thing, Charlotte. I don't care what we call ourselves—Bell, Book or Candle—but nobody is ever to know our real names or find out who we are.

Charlotte We agreed on that.

Emily Because I didn't write for other people to read. They're just rhymes I wrote for myself.

Charlotte I think you know perfectly well they're not just rhymes. They're immeasurably above everything Anne and I have written. Do you think I'm not aware of that? (*Half to herself*) Every time I write a line of my own. (*She stares at Emily, suddenly resenting her*) Why should you write only for yourself?

Emily I'll do what I like!

Charlotte Oh, yes, you'll do what you like. You always have. Nobody in the world is rich enough to buy a share of your solitude.

Emily If I shared it, it would hardly be solitude.

Charlotte You mean you might give some minute part of your precious self away to another human being. You might actually be in danger of turning into somebody else.

Emily looks at her, a little shaken

That's what you're frightened of, isn't it? I remember you in Brussels. Here was the most brilliant, the most gifted man we had ever met and at the very first lesson you had to prove your independence by disagreeing with almost every word he said. (*Unconsciously, her hands grip the locked box in her desk, finally pulling it out*)

Emily I hadn't gone all the way to Brussels to be told to write a little essay in the style of Victor Hugo.

Charlotte Emily Jane Brontë's powerful intellect must remain uncontaminated, of course.

Emily I didn't see any good in his methods, and I still don't.

Charlotte We came away after that first year quite capable of teaching French ourselves.

Emily If I'd learnt to write English the way Monsieur Heger taught us to write French, that's all I'd be *able* to do—teach.

Charlotte We were there to learn from him, not argue. We were the pupils. He was the master.

Emily stares at Charlotte

Emily (*suddenly*) It was Madame Heger.

Charlotte Madame Heger?

Emily Whom you said you wished were dead.

Charlotte What do you mean? Why should I say such a thing? I may have been irritated with her at times. I found her devious and hypocritical. I know that she spied on me. There were no doubt moments when I thought I hated her. (*Bursting out*) I had cause to hate her in my second year there when she deliberately manoeuvred me into saying I would leave, without Monsieur's knowledge, and when he found out he came to me himself . . .

Emily Of course he did. You were a good teacher—he had seen to that.

Charlotte He said I was *not* to go on any account, I was to stay, *he* wished it, and he said as much to her, I have never seen him so angry! He sought me out—when I was alone in the garden—I thought he had gone away and I should never see him again—why should he say that if he didn't care about me? (*She stops short*) It's in no way similar to Branwell's case. Why did you say that? (*She looks at Emily*) You disliked her yourself. (*She holds the box tightly, and Emily glances at it*)

Emily Yes, but I also disliked Monsieur.

Emily stares at Charlotte a moment longer before she turns and goes out, Charlotte looking after her, as—

the Lights fade to a Black-Out

SCENE 2

The same. Night, May 1846

As the Lights go up, Branwell, dishevelled and apparently unconscious, is lying on the sofa in the dining-room, as if he had been thrown there. Nicholls is just closing the front door

Nicholls Yes, it's all right. Thank you. Good night to you. (*In the near dark of the hall he bends to try to clean up some mess on the floor, using first his handkerchief, then taking off his scarf and using that*)

Charlotte, her hair down and her dress partly unbuttoned, comes downstairs, candle in hand, wrapping a shawl around her shoulders

Miss Brontë . . . (*He stares at her for a moment, then awkwardly looks away, disturbed and embarrassed by her appearance*) I'm sorry to . . .
Charlotte Has something happened? What is it?
Reverend Brontë (*off upstairs*) What has happened? Charlotte?
Charlotte It's all right, Papa.
Reverend Brontë (*off*) Is it Branwell?
Charlotte It's Mr Nicholls. It's all right. (*She comes downstairs quickly and into the dining-room, as Nicholls holds the door. She glances at Branwell and lights the lamp*)
Nicholls I fear they've simply thrown him down—without ceremony.
Charlotte No, it's all right.

Charlotte turns Branwell over, straightens him on the sofa without Nicholls' help

Nicholls I—I met them in the lane as they were bringing him home.

Charlotte wipes over Branwell's mouth and chin with her handkerchief

I'm afraid he was—ill—in the hall as we came in.

Branwell mutters a little incoherently

Shall I go for Dr Wheelhouse?
Charlotte Why? I presume they were bringing him from the *Black Bull.*
Nicholls I don't think it's only—what you suppose.

Charlotte unbuttons Branwell's shirt and feels his heart and pulse

Charlotte I doubt if Dr Wheelhouse would thank us for calling him out at such an hour on such an errand.
Nicholls The men seemed to think he'd had some kind of—some kind of fit.
Charlotte (*drily*) I see. A fit.

Branwell stirs again, feeling for the inside pocket of his jacket, and suddenly becoming aware that he is not wearing a jacket

Branwell My jacket.
Charlotte Now lie still.
Branwell I had it on. Where is it?

Charlotte holds him down, glancing at Nicholls

Nicholls He didn't have it when I met him.
Branwell I did. I did have it. I was wearing it! You've stolen it! (*He fights Charlotte's controlling hands with sudden strength*) You've taken my letters!
Nicholls Let me . . .
Charlotte No, no. I'm used to it. (*To Branwell*) Your jacket's at the *Bull*. Now lie down.
Branwell (*throwing her off*) Don't *stop* me, Charlotte!

Anne and Emily appear on the stairs

Branwell gets to his feet and immediately falls against her and back on to the sofa, overcome by dizziness

Nicholls I'll go and fetch it.
Charlotte No—Mr Nicholls—there's no need to . . .

Charlotte looks round to stop Nicholls, as she tends to Branwell, but he is already out of the room

Nicholls goes out the front door

Emily and Anne come down into the dining-room

Now, it's nothing to get alarmed about.

Branwell lies back, exhausted, beginning to cry weakly. Emily removes his boots

Anne He's very white. (*She smooths back his hair*)
Charlotte (*wrapping a rug around him*) He'll be all right after a night's sleep.
Anne (*frightened*) There's blood in his mouth!
Charlotte (*inspecting it*) It's nothing. He's bitten his lip. Bring some water and a clean cloth. (*She draws back a little*) I can assure you that if you go close enough your nose will confirm that the trouble arises from the usual causes.

Anne goes to the kitchen and off

I wonder where he got the money to make such a first-rate job of stupefying himself.

Emily picks up a newspaper and shows her an item in it

When did he see this?
Emily This morning.
Charlotte I'm surprised he didn't hire a horse immediately and ride off to Thorp Green to claim the consolable widow. I suppose we had better batten down the hatches and await the tempest. (*Glancing at Emily*) Nobody warns me of these things, do they?
Emily (*with a shrug*) You were out. Somebody came for him this afternoon.
Charlotte From Thorp Green?
Emily I believe so. Anne knew who it was.
Charlotte And they went off to the *Bull* together?
Emily Presumably.

Anne comes back with a bowl of water and a cloth

Charlotte washes Branwell's face and mouth. He whimpers a little

Charlotte (*to Anne*) Who was it who came from Thorp Green?

Anne glances quickly at Emily to confirm that she has told her

Anne George Gooch.
Charlotte Who is . . . ?
Anne The Robinson's coachman.
Charlotte The coachman. One of Branwell's drinking companions and confidants, no doubt.

Anne is quiet, holding Branwell's hand

Branwell Poor little Branny. Nothing at all . . . Letters.

He whimpers into silence, his grip on Anne's hand loosens. Pause

Charlotte (*wearily*) There's no point in trying to get him upstairs tonight.

In a moment Nicholls returns with Branwell's jacket, knocking on the front door

That's poor Mr Nicholls. (*She goes into the hall*)

Anne and Emily go upstairs

Charlotte lets Nicholls in

That was most kind of you. (*She takes the jacket and seems prepared to dismiss him*)
Nicholls Has he recovered a little?
Charlotte He'll sleep the night through. Unlike the rest of us, probably.
Nicholls Miss Brontë, I . . .

Charlotte looks at him

If it was a—a fit—he—you should put something between his teeth—the tongue—you know, they can bite the tongue.

Charlotte I've no reason to suppose he's had a fit. Why do you keep saying that?

Nicholls It was only—from what they said in the *Bull*, I . . . (*He continues to look at her as if he would tell her more*)

Charlotte (*a little uneasily*) What did they tell you?

Nicholls They said he'd been in a private room with a visitor. Some time after the other man left, they found your brother still in there, unconscious on the floor.

Charlotte And why should they think he'd had a fit?

Nicholls (*embarrassed*) They—doubtless—see your brother from a somewhat different point of view . . .

Charlotte Mr Nicholls, I'm in no position to play the hypocrite with you over this. At the moment my brother is on the brink of disgracing his family still further. There is no reason why you should be the only person in Haworth who doesn't understand the situation.

Nicholls Miss Brontë, do *you* understand the situation?

Charlotte looks at him

Reverend Brontë (*off upstairs*) Charlotte?

Charlotte (*going to the foot of the stairs*) Yes, Papa?

Reverend Brontë (*off*) Is that Branwell?

Charlotte He's home. It's all right. I'll come and see you presently.

Charlotte motions Nicholls into the dining-room and closes the door. Nicholls is again keenly aware of the way she is dressed

My father's curate always holds a privileged position in this household. And you, even more than most, because he is now so inactive.

Nicholls Miss Brontë, I . . . (*He is increasingly moved*)

Charlotte We have no choice but to be open and direct with you. Will you please not talk in riddles? Now, what's been said to you that you're waltzing around so delicately? My brother talks quite freely in the *Black Bull* and naturally there's gossip in the village. Is that what you were referring to?

Nicholls No. No, I . . . Nobody gossips to me.

Charlotte (*her sense of humour breaking through*) Really? Then I'm afraid you must still consider yourself a foreigner in Haworth.

Nicholls (*intensely*) Yes. I feel that I am. Do you see? (*He looks at her fixedly*) A stranger.

Nicholls continues to look at her intensely. Charlotte is suddenly irritated by his gaze, aware he is interpreting her words on another level. She moves further away from him

Charlotte All the same, in common with the rest of the village, you must know about my brother's private affairs. Did they tell you Mr Robinson of Thorp Green has died?

Nicholls (*uneasily*) Yes.

Charlotte Was that the news that led to my brother's "fit"? Did they tell you that?

Nicholls I don't think they—give credence to everything your brother says. They think he—sometimes exaggerates.

Charlotte (*coolly*) I had no idea they were so acute. In the *Bull*.

Nicholls I'm sorry. I . . .

Charlotte Why? Why should you be sorry?

Pause. He stares at her

Nicholls They think he lives in a world which has no existence outside his own imagination.

A moment in which they look at each other, Charlotte suddenly becoming aware of the force of his feelings in a totally new way, moves a little defensively

(*Emotionally*) I would say nothing to cause you pain.

Long pause. Charlotte suddenly draws her wrapper close around her

Miss Brontë, I . . .

Charlotte shakes her head a little, as though to say, "Please go". Nicholls stares at her a moment, then abruptly goes out of the room

Reverend Brontë, coming into sight at the head of the stairs, speaks as Nicholls crosses the hall

Reverend Brontë Charlotte?

Nicholls glances quickly up at him, alarmed by his voice, then goes out through the front door, closing it quietly behind him

Reverend Brontë stands listening on the stairs. In the dining-room Charlotte stands still holding the wrapper close around her. After some moments she goes almost compulsively to bring out her desk, opens it, and takes out the locked box. Reverend Brontë starts to feel his way down the stairs. Charlotte, realizing she has not got the key of the box, comes abruptly out of the dining-room towards the stairs

(*Alarmed*) Who's there?

Charlotte, also taken by surprise, falls back, staring into the darkness of the stairs as if it were Monsieur Heger himself she saw there

Charlotte? (*He reaches the foot of the stairs*)

Charlotte Papa . . .

Reverend Brontë Where are you?

Charlotte comes to take his arm

Charlotte I'm here.

Reverend Brontë Where's Branwell?

Charlotte He's asleep in the dining-room.

Reverend Brontë I'll carry him up to bed.

Charlotte He's comfortable where he is.
Reverend Brontë I could hold him—if you guided me.
Charlotte You're getting cold, standing here.

He submits to being turned and led back to the stairs. Then he stops abruptly, turning suspiciously

I'll put some ointment on your eyes. That will soothe you and help you sleep.
Reverend Brontë He's been sick.
Charlotte He's all right now.
Reverend Brontë I can smell it.
Charlotte Come along.
Reverend Brontë (*shaking off her hand*) Charlotte, will you oblige me by not treating me like a child? Someone came for him today. Who was it?
Charlotte I was out.
Reverend Brontë I heard him speaking in the hall. It didn't sound like a gentleman's voice.
Charlotte Are any of Branwell's "friends" gentlemen?
Reverend Brontë Was it someone from Thorp Green?
Charlotte I wasn't here, Papa.
Reverend Brontë I know you were not here! I am asking you if you know who it was!

Charlotte is silent

(*In growing alarm*) Something's happened. He's not well.

He goes towards the dining-room, miscalculating his direction. Charlotte goes to guide him across to the sofa. She puts his hand lightly on Branwell's heart

Charlotte You see, he's sleeping.

Reverend Brontë kneels by the sofa, his head in his hands, moving restlessly

Reverend Brontë (*abruptly*) I visited Thorp Green, do you know, when you were in Brussels. I still had my sight—I am not usually insensitive to appearances and conversation. And yet I failed completely to divine Mrs Robinson's character from the discourse I had with her.
Charlotte You're getting cold.

She takes his arm and he allows her to help him to his feet

Reverend Brontë If your aunt had not died when she did he would never have fallen prey to this evil woman.
Charlotte Oh, Papa.
Reverend Brontë It's the truth.
Charlotte Whatever happened—it would have made no difference if Aunt had been alive.
Reverend Brontë She gave him something I cannot.
Charlotte She did her duty by us.
Reverend Brontë More than that.

As she is silent, he grows more agitated

It was not easy, Charlotte, to find a second mother for you all. I was still a young man—not yet forty-five. I did indeed make some effort to renew old acquaintances, but . . .

Charlotte Papa, you've nothing to reproach yourself for.

Reverend Brontë I asked—I begged her to stay. I don't know what I should have done if she had said no.

Charlotte Why should she? What else could she do? She was over forty and a spinster.

Reverend Brontë She gave up her life for you all when your mother died.

Charlotte She certainly gave that impression.

Reverend Brontë Why do you say that?

Charlotte Let me take you upstairs to bed.

Reverend Brontë Why do you speak of your aunt in this tone? Charlotte!

Charlotte Papa, she hardly left the house in twenty-one years except to go to church! She never changed the style of her dress or the way she wore her hair from the time she came to Haworth. She shut herself up all day in that room upstairs. If she gave up her life it was her own choice.

Reverend Brontë (*increasingly upset*) You see, Charlotte—you see the difficulty was—the difficulty—she was my wife's sister . . .

Charlotte And that was a call to duty. She told us so a thousand times.

Reverend Brontë She was my wife's sister. She could never be my wife.

Charlotte is so astounded that she laughs

Charlotte Oh, Papa. Of course not. I never knew a more confirmed old maid.

Reverend Brontë Your aunt was a fine woman when I first met her. Spirited and intelligent.

Charlotte With more suitors than any lady in Cornwall. She informed us of the fact herself.

Reverend Brontë You make her a figure of fun—a joke! She was not!

Charlotte Forgive me. We made her a joke, because otherwise some of the things she taught us would have been unendurable.

Reverend Brontë (*shouting*) Was that her fault?

Charlotte (*shocked*) Papa . . .

Reverend Brontë What right have you to criticize her?

Branwell stirs and they both look towards him

(*Lowering his voice*) Do you think life was easy for her? Do you? We had to evolve a way of living together. She usually ate her meals in her room, and I in mine. We met only for a short time each evening. And in this way we were enabled to communicate very well—in a general manner.

Charlotte In a general manner!

Reverend Brontë Do you not understand that we lived together in the same house . . . in close proximity. But real closeness between us would have been a sin against the Church.

Pause

Charlotte I didn't understand. You've never spoken of it . . .
Reverend Brontë How can one speak of such matters? You've no knowledge of what I'm talking about.
Charlotte (*after a pause*) No . . .
Reverend Brontë I should not want you to have. (*Pause*) It is frequently
right and necessary that the natural feelings which arise between a man
and a woman should be suppressed. (*His control breaks as he goes on*)
It is this that distorts, do you not see? The force that builds up within
the confines of the body. The great enemy trapped in the flesh—without
escape—across the years. And what once was pure and good in God's
eyes becomes corruption—takes possession, as the cancer possessed your
mother's sweet body before she died.

She reaches out to him and he clings to her

If you'd known your mother—the way she looked at me when we first
met, in her uncle's drawing-room, so direct, so true, it went through my
heart . . . On our wedding night she came to me full of joy, without
shame, like an opening flower. (*He clings to her, overcome with emotion*)
Charlotte I understand—Papa . . .

*He seems to become aware of himself and draws away from her, reserve
falling on him like a cloak*

I understand.

He pushes away, making his own way across the room, feeling for the door

Papa . . .

Reverend Brontë goes out of the room and upstairs

Charlotte stands isolated, as the Lights fade to Black-Out

Scene 3

The same. Morning, two days later

*Anne is in the dining-room, sewing. Emily is in the kitchen, baking. After
some moments, Branwell creeps downstairs, almost on all fours. His hair
is a wild mop, his shirt hangs outside his breeches, his feet are bare, he seems
to have physically shrunk. He lingers outside the kitchen door for some
moments watching Emily, who takes no notice. Finally Branwell moves into
the room. Emily silently fetches him a bowl of porridge from the outer kitchen,
cuts him slices of bread and meat, sets them before him, much as if she were
feeding one of the dogs. Branwell sits at the table staring at the food as Emily
goes back to her bread-making. Branwell begins to eat the bread and meat
hungrily, but soon falters. He frequently rubs his eyes. He takes up the*

carving knife Emily has left beside the joint of meat and begins to play with it, rubbing a finger along the blade

Charlotte comes downstairs and into the kitchen. She looks at Branwell and he grips the knife to him possessively

Branwell I need it in case I meet the devil.

Charlotte sorts out some ironed-laundry on the table. Branwell advances on Emily with the knife, grips her from behind, trying to force the knife between her clenched teeth

Emily Jane, the intrepid knife-swallower!

Charlotte hesitates. Emily pushes the knife away and calmly continues shaping loaves from the dough

Emily I don't like the taste.

Branwell puts the knife down. In a moment he picks up the poker, Charlotte observing him

Branwell Perhaps you would prefer it if I put out your eyes with the red-hot poker?

Emily No. I don't care for the sizzling noise as the eyeballs melt.

Branwell The brains boiling and bubbling in the cranium—the bone cracking in little sharp spurts . . . Whish! The blood trickling like communion wine—only a mouthful at a time to the vampires at the altar rail.

Pause

Emily Besides, if you put my eyes out I couldn't see to bake the bread.

Branwell, reminded of his own disabilities, drops the poker, rubbing his eyes

Charlotte (*to Emily*) Tabby's consented to spend the day in bed for once. After a great deal of grumbling.

Charlotte goes out to the back with the pile of laundry

Branwell Sometimes I think I'm going blind. What if Papa died and I was blind, what in heaven or hell would become of me?

Emily I expect you'd be a sort of disreputable cripple on the parish. (*She finishes shaping loaves, slides the tray into the oven, calmly moving him out of the way. Then she starts to clean up the table*)

Branwell You could go out to work, I dare say, and support me.

Emily hesitates a little over her work

Or are we to go on the parish together?

Emily scrubs at the table vigorously

What *would* you do? If Papa died? He might die this summer. The operation could kill him.

Pause. Emily does not show that she has heard him. Branwell's appeal is increasingly anxious

Would you go out as a governess?

Pause. Emily begins to scrub the table again with unnecessary vigour

Wouldn't it be agreeable if we could write together again? Publish our novels together as one work in three volumes. By Branwell and Emily Brontë. (*He pictures the title with his hand*) I'll go to London personally. I still have good contacts in the literary world, you know, who will give me introductions. I shall take our manuscripts to the best publishers in England, and I shall lay them on the desk—What is your best offer? And if they can't do better than that, well then, there are plenty of others who will snap it up like that! (*He clicks his fingers*)

Pause. Emily goes on with her job, her face showing unwanted anxiety. Branwell watches her in silent appeal for some moments, but Emily does not look at him

Shall I tell you what happened when I went to London last time?
Emily You were robbed of all your money.
Branwell No. I wasn't robbed. I lost it—or gave it away, or spent it, or— I don't know—quite—what.

Emily looks at him and stops her work

I remember every detail of the beginning—but the end isn't clear in my mind at all. (*Pause*) Except one night a man I'd met on the coach took me out and we went to some house, I don't know where it was. It seemed to me almost as grand as the Duke of Wellington's. And there was a woman in a room with silk wallpaper, lying on a bed dressed in a velvet robe. Green and blue. Peacock colours. At first in the candlelight her hair looked soft and fair on the pillow, and the skin of her arms like cream. Then, afterwards . . . (*He stops abruptly. Pause. Emotionally*) All the pleasure is in the anticipation—do you see? So anxious and impatient and incomplete . . . Is this *all* that is to be?

Pause. Emily stays with her hand resting on the table, not looking at him (*Quietly*) Please help me.

Emily I can't. (*Pause. She wipes over the table again, not looking at him*)

In a moment Branwell settles back in his chair, trembling

Emily goes out to the back kitchen with the cloth and bowl, her face showing unwonted anxiety and conflict

In a moment Branwell goes out of the room, taking a rough sandwich of bread and meat with him. He goes into the dining-room. Anne looks up from her sewing. Branwell goes to lie on the sofa, slipping into the Northangerland rôle he puts on in her presence like a change of coat

Branwell (*indicating the sandwich*) The first food to pass my lips for two days and it tastes like old flannel.

Anne You slept all day yesterday.

Branwell Did I? I wept all night. "Weeping may endure for a night but joy cometh in the morning." Beware the words of the Holy Writ, for they juggle with us like the blasted witches on the blasted heath.

Anne Dr Wheelhouse came while you were asleep.

Branwell Now there's a man who could instruct the devil in his work.

Anne He's a good man. He wants you to get well.

Branwell Oh, yes. he's a good man. I'm postulating that he'll be up there with the rest of you while I'm on my way down below. (*He puts on his Yorkshire accent*) "Has he coom yet?" "Who?" "Him. Young Brontë." "Not yet. The fire's not hot enough yet." (*He stops at Anne's distress*) It's nothing but a highly coloured old fable, you know—perpetuated to keep the lower orders in their places.

Anne You don't believe that.

Branwell Don't I? Well, if I'm wrong I shall have you up there to plead for me.

Anne *I* can't plead for you.

Branwell Why not? I'm counting on it.

Anne You must do it yourself.

Branwell If you don't plead for me I shall be doomed. (*In a choked voice*) Doomed! (*He suddenly jerks his head as if the noose has just tightened around his neck*)

Anne (*in a low voice*) If I thought there was no hope for you, I should hardly want to live myself.

Branwell stares at her, suddenly outraged by the guilt she instils in him

Branwell Now why say that? Holy Mary, mother of—whoever it was. Why are you *always* like this? (*He indicates her helplessly*) This—doormat that I can't resist stamping on with my dirty boots.

Anne I want to help you . . .

Branwell Why me? Why not your*self*? Why don't you ever reach out and *grab* something from life?

Anne I can't. How can I?

Charlotte enters and comes through to the hall

Branwell What if you're the one that's wrong? And this *is* all there is? A thousand million times worse than the other thing. The realms of glory are *here*, every day of your life means one less day to find them, and even as you're about to reach out for them—every time—they— (*he gestures hopelessly*)—go up in a puff of smoke.

Charlotte comes quietly into the room as he speaks. In a moment Branwell resumes to Anne in careful, artificial tones again, but now mostly for Charlotte's benefit

Perhaps what hell means is that Mr Edmund Robinson and I shall find

ourselves roasting on spits over adjacent fires. He's there at this moment,
I dare say, reducing down some of that flabby fat into one of Old Nick's
dripping tins.

Anne (*in a low voice*) It isn't for us to judge him.

Branwell *I'll* judge him. I have the right. He hated me.

Anne He didn't. Even if he did . . .

Branwell He has contrived to reach out from the grave itself to keep us
apart.

*Charlotte glances at him, observing as she did in the kitchen. She settles in
a chair with her darning*

My heart almost burst when George Gooch told me how she is suffering.
She cannot sleep or eat—she kneels in her bedroom day and night in
bitter tears and prayers.

Charlotte (*without looking up*) Why?

Branwell looks at her

I thought you were both praying night and day for her husband's death.
She seems remarkably hard to please.

Pause

Branwell You don't even want to understand, do you?

Charlotte Yes, Branwell. I want to understand.

Branwell Do you suppose she is unmoved by her husband's death—when
she has worn herself out in attendance on him? Do you imagine she is
not tortured by conscience? By searing agonies of guilt and remorse?

Charlotte Why? (*Pause*) Remorse over what?

Branwell You have no knowledge of life whatever!

Charlotte Then tell me about it. Give me that knowledge.

Branwell If you knew the depth of our feelings for one another . . . if you
read her letters . . .

Charlotte She writes to you?

Branwell (*holding his jacket*) Of course. I carry them on my person always.
I shall die with them next to my heart.

*Pause. Charlotte looks intently at him, and Branwell finally turns away from
her gaze to Anne, who lowers her eyes. A few moments of silence in which
Branwell's frustrations come to boiling point. He suddenly gets up abruptly*

I cannot *endure* this atmosphere of disapproval and distrust! You don't
seem to care a pin about me at the very moment when—I've lost the
one person who does care and understand and love me.

Their failure to respond adds to his despair

I've no escape. I have no means or powerful friends. How can I be
expected to write without the least encouragement or support?

Charlotte How can any of us write without these things? We none of us
have them. Are you special in some way—set apart from the rest of us?

Branwell You give encouragement to Emily . . . Don't think I haven't

heard you. When you all read your novels to each other in here in the
evening . . . No praise is too high for *her*! (*He says it as a child would
say it*)

Charlotte Because I see worth in Emily! I see pure gold flowing out as
though nothing in the world could hold it back. How could I be true
to myself if I did not praise Emily? Do you think it's easy for *me*? When
my own efforts halt and limp on to the page . . .

Branwell You've read nothing of mine for years.

Charlotte I've read nothing because you show us nothing. We don't see
you working. We simply hear you talk about it.

Branwell (*staring at her*) You don't *believe* me, do you?

Charlotte I don't know what to believe, Branwell.

Branwell You honestly do not believe a single word I say.

Charlotte turns away from him

Very well, Charlotte. Very well. You just wait here. I'll fetch my novel.
Don't go away. You can read my novel. You wait here, Charlotte.

Branwell storms out and up the stairs in a blaze of self-delusive anger

*Charlotte darns fiercely for a few moments before she looks up at Anne, who
is watching her*

Charlotte Is this the way you talked when you were together at Thorp Green?

Anne looks at her as if she doesn't understand her question

As you were talking now when I came into the room.

Anne Yes, I suppose . . . Yes.

Charlotte He confided in you.

Anne Yes.

Charlotte You've told us so little. You talk in monosyllables. You don't
talk. You listen.

Anne He needed someone to listen!

Charlotte But what was it *like*? When did you see each other?

Anne Usually in the evening. For an hour or two. After the children were
in bed. I thought . . . (*She hesitates*)

Charlotte Yes? Tell me. What did you think?

Anne That if he knew that I was—always there—he would come, no
matter what had happened—as to a sanctuary.

Charlotte (*straining to hear*) "As to a . . . ?" I can't hear you, my love.

Emily comes into the kitchen

Anne A sanctuary. (*Her voice falters as she meets Charlotte's eyes*)

Charlotte stares at her with new insight

*Branwell comes downstairs with the manuscript. He comes into the dining-
room and sweeps it down in front of Charlotte*

Branwell (*in a Yorkshire accent*) There thou'art. (*At top speed*) Into thy hands I commend it, and you may say what you please about it, provided you acknowledge it is a work of genius.

Branwell sweeps out of the room, and out the front door, in a state of feverish excitement

Emily from the kitchen door observes him go. She comes to the dining-room door, observing Charlotte with the manuscript. Anne's anxious look meets hers. Emily occupies herself in the room, dusting or tidying. They both covertly watch Charlotte pick up the manuscript and look at the first page, leaf over to the second. Charlotte suddenly throws it aside with contempt. Anne looks at Emily in mounting anxiety. Emily's face also begins again to betray anxious involvement. Charlotte is too absorbed in her own thoughts to be aware of them

Emily (*abruptly*) When are they sending the books?
Charlotte (*not with her*) What books?
Emily The poems. (*With contempt*) Currer, Ellis and Acton Bell.
Charlotte Perhaps they'll come this month. The publishers said May in their last letter, didn't they?
Emily He mustn't see them. Write to the publishers.
Charlotte They're probably already on their way.
Emily We must tell the post office to hold the parcel until we collect it.
Charlotte (*picking up the manuscript again*) It would mean nothing to him, even if he did see them. He lives in a dream.
Emily (*staring at her*) I'll write to them myself.

Emily walks out of the room, and exits through the kitchen

Charlotte leafs through the manuscript as she talks to Anne, in a growing excitement which frightens her sister

Charlotte He always came to your schoolroom? You never went to the house where he lodged?
Anne No.
Charlotte And then he'd tell you what had happened to him during the day?
Anne (*nodding; almost inaudibly*) Yes.
Charlotte And I suppose sometimes he told you things that shocked and disgusted you . . . ?
Anne I didn't ever stop him!
Charlotte No matter how hard he tried? That's what he used to do when we were children—do you remember? It wouldn't take him long then to have you in tears.
Anne As a child I didn't know when he was telling the truth and when he . . .
Charlotte (*after a slight pause*) And you do know now?
Anne You don't understand what these people at Thorp Green are like!

Charlotte Well, tell me! What *are* they like? Nobody ever has told me in plain terms.

Anne A woman like that gets hold of someone as vulnerable as Branwell and corrupts him utterly. I *do* tell you. You don't understand the malice, the depravity of these people.

Charlotte You see you use words like corruption and depravity and sin. You don't tell me what actually took place.

Anne They dragged him down to their level. I couldn't do anything about it except stay on and hope my influence might prevail a little against hers . . .

Charlotte Like a duel—for his soul.

Anne I might have prevailed! If I'd had the strength to stay—if I hadn't let him talk me into leaving when I did. You see I *wanted* to leave—I thought of myself, not him—I only wanted to get away—to be home—in peace.

Charlotte My dear . . .

Anne I should never, never have brought him to that house in the first place.

Charlotte Why did you? If it was such a den of iniquity.

Anne Do you think I would have got him the situation if I'd realized? Before he came? *I'm* the one who's guilty.

Charlotte How could you be guilty? If you didn't know before he came?

Anne seems close to tears

But how did you know *after* he came? If you were almost always in the schoolroom with your charges—how did you *know* what went on in the rest of the house?

Anne The older girls used to come and confide in me.

Charlotte But did they tell you about Branwell and their mother?

Anne Of course not. They knew nothing about it.

Charlotte Because its very essence was secrecy and guilt.

Anne Nothing in that house was what it seemed on the surface.

Charlotte Then how *did* you know?

Anne Well, of course, because he told me!

Pause. Charlotte stares at her. Anne, wrought up, sweeps on, as if the barriers to her speech were down at last

I don't believe God would condemn any of his creatures for ever. The Bible says it again and again: "He that is able to subdue all things to Himself will have all men to be saved." When I was young I found about thirty passages which say the same thing in one way or another, and I showed them to Aunt, and she said there were as many to prove otherwise, but it isn't true.

Charlotte Annie . . .

Anne And do you know that the word they translate as eternal doesn't mean that at all in the original Greek: it means for *ages*, not for *ever*. No-one is condemned *for ever*!

Charlotte Of course not! You can't still believe in such a God?

Anne (*in a low voice*) I'm afraid. (*She looks up at Charlotte, agonized*) For Branwell. I still have nightmares about it. The lake of unquenchable fire. At Thorp Green I used to wake up in the night in terror. And in the dark I would think I was in bed again in Aunt's room—so hot and close—stifling me—and I'd lie there trying to breathe. (*Her breathing begins to falter as she speaks*)
Charlotte Aunt's God is an impostor—a bogey to frighten naughty children.
Anne But there's no *proof*. Do you see?
Charlotte You just gave me proof.
Anne I can't get the fear out of my mind. I cannot endure to see him—cast away.
Charlotte But is he really so wicked?

Anne looks at her, uncomprehending

Oh, I know his faults. But what are his sins?

Anne stares at her

You still haven't told me.
Anne You know about Mrs Robinson!
Charlotte Do I? I know a character you and Branwell have created for us. I suspect she's in his novel. But that doesn't constitute a sin. Except perhaps against the reader. (*Quickly*) Oh, my love. These are childhood fantasies. Dreams. They hold you back from . . . achieving anything at all.

Branwell comes in at the front door

(*Rising*) Branwell?
Anne Charlotte . . .
Charlotte (*going to the door*) Branwell?

Anne follows Charlotte and stands behind her

Emily appears at the kitchen door

Branwell What's this? A committee of welcome? (*He throws his jacket open*) I hold no concealed bottles or contraband.
Charlotte Come in here.
Anne Branwell . . .

Charlotte looks at her. Anne begins to cough or struggle for breath

Branwell Poor old misery.
Charlotte Lie down for a while, Annie. Go upstairs and rest.
Anne Why? Why should I go upstairs? I'm quite well.
Charlotte (*urgently*) Anne, please go when I tell you! I'm sorry, but you simply haven't the strength. (*She holds the door open*)

Anne, looking at Branwell who appears quite uninterested, goes into the hall.

She would stop and talk to Emily, while still struggling against the oncoming asthmatic attack, but Emily seems unaware of her

    Emily goes out through the kitchen. Anne exits upstairs

Branwell goes to sprawl on the dining-room sofa

Branwell They wouldn't serve me in the *Bull*. It seems old Arthur Martha Nicholls put the fear of God into them the other night. It's the first time I've ever known a publican turn down ready money. It's almost as incredible as if they handed you back your sixpence from the collection plate in church.

Charlotte Perhaps they reckon the circumstance of your having ready money isn't likely to arise very often.

Branwell You don't think I'm going to make my fortune as a novelist, then?

Charlotte (*going to sit across from him*) Branwell, you must face the fact that you will never see this woman again.

Pause. He is a little shaken, taken by surprise

    I know it's painful. But there's no point in building castles in the air.

Branwell I'm not building castles in the air!

Charlotte She cares nothing for you.

Branwell She is suffering the tortures of the damned at this very moment.

Charlotte Then why don't you go to her? Why doesn't she come to you?

Branwell How can she?

Charlotte I thought you'd go flying off to Thorp Green the minute you heard.

Branwell I can't go. It would be too dangerous. She warned me to stay away.

Charlotte How could it be dangerous?

Branwell She is surrounded by people of power and influence—men who could crush us both, as easily as you might crush a spider.

Charlotte Who do you mean? What men?

Branwell It isn't Haworth, you know. The daily society at Thorp Green doesn't consist of the curate and the sexton.

Charlotte Well, whoever they are, how do they have the right to tell Mrs Robinson what she is to do, and who she is to see?

Branwell My dear Charlotte. Has it occurred to you that you may not be in possession of all the facts?

Charlotte Perhaps you would take pity on my ignorance.

Branwell seems to be controlling his irritation with difficulty

Branwell I see no reason why I should.

Charlotte And plenty of reasons why you shouldn't. Facts are such hard, tangible objects, are they not? Likely to bring castles in the air crashing down around one's ears. (*She turns away to find her work-basket, as if the conversation were over*)

Branwell There is the small matter of the will.
Charlotte The will?
Branwell My dear Charlotte, it is by this time common knowledge that Mr Edmund Robinson has provided in his will that if—if his widow has any communication whatever with yours truly here—she will not get one penny of his estate. Not one penny. She is rendered powerless. Is that "fact" enough for you?

He meets Charlotte's searching gaze with new confidence

Laugh if you must. I admit it seems like a macabre joke—a page from the Devil's Jestbook. I dare not go near her—she would be ruined.
Charlotte How do you know this?
Branwell News of it has come from all sides. One of the executors has already said that if he sees me he will blow my brains out.
Charlotte And you are frightened to go to her?
Branwell Oh, for God's sake. Do you think I care what bodily risks I run?
Charlotte Then it is she who will not risk losing her fortune for your sake?
Branwell She hasn't only herself to consider. She has children.
Charlotte Are you telling me the will deprives the whole family of their patrimony if the mother remarries?
Branwell It doesn't forbid her to remarry! It is designed specifically to prevent her marriage to *me*.
Charlotte What an extraordinary clause to put in a will. I wonder how it could possibly be phrased.
Branwell I dare say with his diabolical cunning he employed the best lawyers money can buy.
Charlotte And you said she would pay the forfeit if she held any communication with you whatever?
Branwell Yes.
Charlotte So she can't even write to you?
Branwell Only in secret.
Charlotte And if it is discovered the entire family will be cut off without a penny. I wonder where the money will go then? Perhaps some worthy charitable institution will have reason to be very grateful to you.
Branwell It's exceedingly funny, isn't it?
Charlotte Perhaps incredible would be a more appropriate word.
Branwell I don't know all the *details*. It mightn't be *exactly* in these terms but . . .
Charlotte But in *general* that is the situation?
Branwell (*lamely*) It's the only possible explanation.

He meets her gaze and looks away, as if caught out. Pause

Charlotte It sounds like a chapter from one of your stories.
Branwell Possibly that's because my stories are written from life.
Charlotte Oh.
Branwell (*glancing at the manuscript*) Have you read any of the opus yet?
Charlotte All I need to.

Pause

Branwell You know, there are times when you couldn't be anything but a
schoolmistress. (*He presses on the tender nerve*) Have you heard from
your mentor lately?

Charlotte Who?

Branwell Whatsisname—your Belgian professor—Monsewer God Almighty Heger.

Charlotte's expression tightens. She pushes the manuscript across to him

Very well then. The Truth Severe. What comments do you intend to
make?

Charlotte None.

Branwell Does that mean you consider it beyond and above criticism?

Charlotte It means I don't intend to comment.

Branwell Or is it that you prefer to wait until the work is complete for
fear of impeding the young genius's free flow of thought?

Charlotte You choose whichever explanation pleases you.

Branwell I'd like the true one.

Charlotte Oh, no, Branwell. The truth is not what you want.

Branwell (*staring at her*) I can't tell you—what you looked like—as you
said that. Do you *know* what you look like these days?

Charlotte I have a mirror.

Branwell Your whole face has changed. It used to be full of interest—
sensitive to everything I said. And you used to laugh a lot. Now it's a
—stiletto. God Almighty! I want to know what you *think*. (*His voice
begins to tremble*) Once we discussed everything together. We encouraged
each other.

Charlotte I encouraged *you*.

Branwell We helped one another.

Charlotte Branwell, all our lives were built around you! I took my first
situation as a teacher so there'd be money for *you* to go to London.

Branwell Nobody made you. You wanted to.

Charlotte I *wanted* to, yes! My one ambition in life was your success.

Branwell Then help me *now*.

She turns away. Pause

(*Recovering himself*) Imagine you are the Great Panjandrum himself in
the schoolroom at Brussels and I am your humble pupil. No, I am *you*.
(*Imitating her*) "Oh, Master, Master, let me hear your voice once more.
Say to me what you will—but for pity's sake, say *something* . . ."

Charlotte looks at him sharply, surprised and alarmed

"The six months of silence have run their course."

Charlotte You've been at my papers!

Branwell (*shrugging*) If you leave them lying around, for all to see . . .

Charlotte I keep them under lock and key. (*Greatly disturbed, she goes to
get her desk*)

Branwell I've shown you my novel. Am I not to be admitted to the secrets of your heart and mind?

Charlotte (*opening the desk*) You must have been very quick. When I was called in to Papa—or someone at the door . . . (*She takes out the box, unlocks it with the key she carries on her, anxiously checks that the bundle of letters is intact*)

Branwell I didn't take anything. (*He is momentarily in complete command again*)

Charlotte takes out the half-written letter with the same anxious absorption. Finally she meets Branwell's ironic gaze. Long pause

Come, then. *You* are *he.* Whose granite heart the most piteous letter cannot touch. You have read my novel. Now cometh the Judgement.

Pause. Charlotte, now very angry, stands looking at him, still holding her letter in her hand

Charlotte (*at length*) Very well. Given those circumstances, I imagine I would say—(*she pauses momentarily*)—that it's no good at all. That it's rubbish from beginning to end—a waste of your time in writing and mine in reading it. That it has no characterization, no skill in construction, no insight into human behaviour, no reality. You ask for the truth and there it is!

Pause

Branwell You haven't even had time to read it.

Charlotte I've read it a hundred times in the past!

Branwell That's a lie. It's totally new.

Charlotte It's the same old Glasstown story dished up yet again, with Northangerland as the hero . . .

Branwell (*his voice trembling*) I've read sections of it to certain chosen friends, and they happen to have praised it very highly indeed. Lydia believes I have talent of an exceedingly high order.

Charlotte Is that why you think she loves you? Because she praises you?

Branwell I've never needed to think that.

Charlotte The mere fact that you feel very deeply about another person doesn't *make* that person care about you. You *feel* it must . . . The mere force of your own feelings . . . But it doesn't.

Branwell I have proof enough that she cares.

Charlotte What proof? Everything you've told me so far proves to me that she doesn't care one jot for you. *What proof?*

Branwell Do you suppose I'm going to tell you everything that's passed between us?

Charlotte Branwell, I must *know.*

Branwell Why?

Charlotte Because I *need* to!

Branwell again stares at her insolently

You might have built a whole world on something she felt only for a moment. Do you see?

Branwell shakes his head confidently

Or on an expression of feeling she makes to many people. Not you alone.

Branwell (*emotionally*) What do you think she is? A London whore? (*Pause*) Are you unable to believe that ladies of elegance and beauty can also be good, pure women?

Charlotte Oh, God, help us—what is a good, pure woman? One of the stone effigies in York Cathedral? I don't feel I have much in common with them.

Branwell I didn't know we were talking about *you.*

Charlotte again turns from his stare, still grasping the letter to her, half-unconsciously

Charlotte She was flirting—playing with you.

Branwell Why do you think such a woman would keep me by her at all costs, if she did not more than reciprocate my deep feelings for her?

Charlotte Yes. Why? Do you see? Why didn't she send you away? Let you go. You ask yourself again and again. Why did they say this or that —or look at you as if your presence in the room was all they cared about, or give you little unexpected gifts—or press your hand . . . (*She stops momentarily*) Perhaps it flatters them—to have someone so patently miserable for their sake, so pathetically grateful for every kindness. So totally enslaved. They give just enough to nourish your dreams—the long constant hazy ones, and the little sharp sudden visions of you both together, until the day comes when you become an embarrassment to them, and then . . . (*She sweeps her hand across, as to say "finish"*) Because in reality there is no comfort for you there, no companionship, no security, no love.

Pause

Branwell Do you seriously believe that what lies between Lydia and myself bears any resemblance to your pathetic schoolgirl attachment to this— conceited little Belgian?

Pause

Charlotte You can't see this woman straight, as other people see her.

Branwell My dear girl, if you were not seeing life through a distorting glass of major dimensions at this very moment, you would not be standing there wondering whether to post that letter or not. He won't reply to it, you know. Not ever.

Pause. They stare at each other

Do you suppose that what Lydia has given of herself to me could be closed up in a little box such as you have there. Love is *giving*—not withholding. Her emotion and passion pour forth with such generosity and wealth that heaven itself cannot encompass them.

Pause. He merges into his dream

Do you think I haven't been to see her alone time and time again—in the room with silk wallpaper—where she lies on the bed dressed in a velvet robe. Blue and green. Peacock colours. And her soft golden hair falls over the pillow . . .
Charlotte (*staring at him*) I thought her hair was dark.
Branwell What?
Charlotte You said her "golden hair". Doesn't it matter to you?

Branwell seems momentarily confused and vulnerable

Branny—tell me the truth. You must tell me.
Branwell *I don't* understand what you want! (*He looks as if he would escape out of the room, and is pushed back by realities*) If they're not going to take my money at the *Bull*, what the hell am I going to do?

Pause. His mind seems to focus again. He pulls some letters partly out of his pocket

Branwell I have her letters. Are those real enough for you?
Charlotte Show me.

He keeps his hand across them

I can't see when you hold them like that.
Branwell Holy Jesu, do you actually need to see where the ink is smudged by her tears . . . (*He pushes them back in his pocket*)
Charlotte Branwell, you must show them to me.
Branwell They're love letters.
Charlotte How do you know?
Branwell How do I *know*? (*He laughs*)
Charlotte You might be reading some meaning into them she never intended. You can always find a code. I could make a love letter out of a laundry list!

They stare at each other. Charlotte as if she must divine the solution to her own problems in Branwell's eyes. He passes his hand over his face, as if fighting the clouds pressing in on his mind

Are they old letters? Has she stopped writing altogether? But even then you persuade yourself it is only because they care. Any reason but the one truth that explains all. Branny, they don't care a fraction of a pin! Their feelings haven't changed—they never existed. You have taken the extraordinary liberty of loving where it was not asked.
Branwell But she *hasn't* stopped writing. *I* still get letters. George Gooch carries them between us.

He takes the letters from his pocket again and puts them on the table. Pause. Charlotte's attention is suddenly caught by the writing on the top envelope

Charlotte Branwell, that's *your* writing . . . (*She looks through the letters in growing excitement*)

Branwell is too confused and dazed to stop her

These are *your* letters to her. Half of them haven't even been opened. Is this what George Gooch brought when he came the other day?
Branwell Yes . . . No, no—I—showed you the wrong ones. (*He feels vaguely through his pockets*)
Charlotte She's never written to you, has she?
Branwell Yes!
Charlotte Branny, there's nothing. It doesn't exist. Look at them. *Look.* You made it all up out of your own imagination.
Branwell No, Charlotte—I didn't. (*He begins to whimper a little*)
Charlotte There won't be any more letters. It's over.
Branwell No—Charlotte . . .
Charlotte It never existed. You invented the whole thing.
Branwell No, Charlotte—I didn't! I didn't, Charlotte . . . (*He is crying*) She cares what becomes of me. She does care!
Charlotte (*oblivious*) No reply will come. Ever. (*She is crumpling the letter in her hand*) You're free. (*She seems to become aware of what she is doing, to the letter, laughs involuntarily, and throws it in the basket, totally unaware of the intensity of his distress. She takes up the bundle of Heger's letters and unties the special ribbon which binds them, as if she would consign them to the same fate*)
Branwell Charlotte! I didn't, Charlotte—I didn't—make it up . . .
Charlotte Simply forget. It's dead. (*With decision, she replaces the letters in the box and goes to the door with it*)

Branwell, unnoticed, calls after her

Branwell Charlotte! She *cares*!

Charlotte goes out, letting the door bang shut behind her. Branwell sinks to the floor near the sofa. Charlotte goes to where her coat or shawl is hanging in the hall

Emily comes to the kitchen door, watching Charlotte

Charlotte puts the box on a chair and puts on the shawl or coat. Emily goes through to the dining-room, unnoticed, and looks at Branwell, helpless on the floor. Charlotte picks up the box, locking it decisively. Emily comes to the dining-room door, watching her in amazement. Charlotte becomes aware of her

Charlotte Oh, hullo! I'm going for a walk. It's so fresh after the storm last night. The waterfall will be magnificent. I shall be gone some time. I want to bury something on the moors.

Charlotte exits through the front door

Emily is too stunned to speak until the door shuts behind Charlotte

Emily (*moving*) Charlotte! What about . . . ? (*Her head indicates Branwell in the dining-room, but Charlotte has gone*)

Emily glances in again at Branwell. He is whimpering as a dog whimpers, physically and emotionally helpless. Emily goes to the foot of the stairs, hesitates again, looking back at the dining-room door, then finally calls up the stairs

(*In a low voice*) Anne?

There is no reply. Emily does not try again, but in a moment goes back to the dining-room, looking at Branwell. Finally she goes in and gets him up and on to the sofa, capably, as she might a sick animal, Branwell crying and clinging to her like a child

Branwell She *does* care . . .

As Emily starts to leave him he reaches for her and grips her, so that she is imprisoned. She tries to escape, then finally puts her hand on his head to comfort him, as—

the CURTAIN *falls*

FURNITURE AND PROPERTY LIST

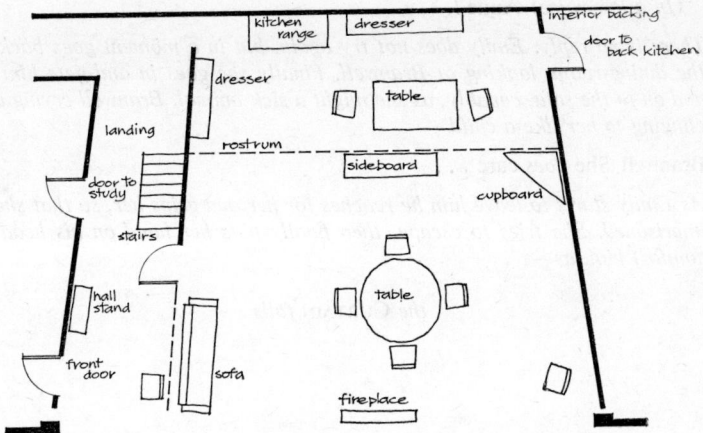

ACT I

SCENE 1

On stage: DINING-ROOM
  Circular table. *On it:* cloth, oil lamp
  4 small chairs
  Armchair
  Sofa
  Sideboard. *On it:* work-basket containing stockings; 3 writing desks
      with writing materials, notebooks, pens, and (in **Charlotte**'s) small
      box with letters tied with silk and loose sheets of paper; white
      tablecloth
  Corner cupboard
  In fireplace: fire-irons

  KITCHEN
  2 dressers. *On them:* crockery, general kitchen dressing
  Range. *On it:* pots, pans, general kitchen dressing
      Beside it: poker
  Table
  2 chairs

HALL
Hall-stand
Chair

LANDING
Clock
Carpets
Stair carpet

Off stage: Small travelling bag (**Anne**)
2 larger travelling bags (**Branwell**)
Tray of soup in plates, side plates, soup spoons, bread, butter, cheese,
knives, cups, saucers, teapot, milk, sugar bowl, teaspoons (**Emily**)

SCENE 2

Strike: All meal dishes and tray
Socks

Set: Map on table
Notebook and pencil on table
Reset table chairs

Off stage: Travelling box (**Emily**)

SCENE 3

Strike: Box from hall
Map from table

Set: Tray of cups on kitchen table
2 desks from sideboard to table
Vegetables in bowl, dish, knife on kitchen table

Personal: **Charlotte:** Watch, key on chain

ACT II

SCENE 1

Strike: Desks, etc., back to sideboard

Set: Pail and brush in kitchen
Newspaper on table
Bag (for clothes) beside sideboard
Anne's sewing on table

Off stage: Sealed letter **(Stage Management** as Postman)
               Bundle of clothes including man's woollen drawers **(Charlotte)**

SCENE 2

Strike: Desk back to sideboard
               Anne's sewing to sideboard
               Newspaper

Off stage: Candle **(Anne)**
               Bowl of water and cloth **(Anne)**

Personal: **Nicholls:** handkerchief, scarf
               Charlotte: handkerchief

SCENE 3

Strike: Bowl and cloth
               Candle

Set: Dough and bowl and tray for breadmaking on kitchen table
               Bread, bread knife and board on kitchen dresser
               Meat on plate and knife on kitchen dresser
               Laundry on kitchen table
               Cloth and bowl on kitchen dresser
               Anne's sewing on dining-room table
               Charlotte's darning in work-basket on sideboard
               Duster in sideboard drawer
               Charlotte's shawl on hall-stand

Off stage: Bowl of porridge **(Emily)**
               Manuscript **(Branwell)**
               Packet of letters **(Branwell)**

LIGHTING PLOT

Property fittings required: 3 oil table lamps
A dining-room, hall and kitchen. The same scene throughout

ACT I, SCENE 1. Night

To open: All lamps lit

Cue 1   **Anne:** "Nothing's the matter."   (Page 16)
          Fade to Black-Out

ACT I, SCENE 2. Night

To open: As Scene 1

Cue 2   **Charlotte:** ". . . through the nights!"   (Page 24)
          Fade to Black-Out

ACT I, SCENE 3. Night

To open: As Scene 1

No cues

ACT II, SCENE 1. Day

To open: General effect of morning light

Cue 3   **Emily** exits   (Page 49)
          Fade to Black-Out

ACT II, SCENE 2. Night

To open: Kitchen and dining-room lamps off: hall lamp dimly lit

Cue 4   **Charlotte** lights dining-room lamp   (Page 50
          Bring up dining-room lamp and covering lighting

Cue 5   **Reverend Brontë** goes upstairs   (Page 57)
          Fade to Black-Out

ACT II, SCENE 3. Day

To open: As Scene 1

No cues

EFFECTS PLOT

ACT I

SCENE 1

No cues

SCENE 2

No cues

SCENE 3

No cues

ACT II

SCENE 1

Cue 1   **Tabby:** ". . . for Master's supper."   (Page 37)
             Postman's knock

SCENE 2

No cues

SCENE 3

No cues